The Capacity to Love

The Capacity to Love

JACK DOMINIAN

Darton Longman & Todd
London

First published 1985 by
Darton Longman & Todd Ltd
89 Lillie Road, London SW6 1UD

Reprinted 1986

© 1985 Jack Dominian

ISBN 0 232 51643 X

British Library Cataloguing in Publication Data

Dominian, Jack
  The capacity to love.
  1. Love (Theology)
  I. Title
  248.4   BV4639

ISBN 0–232–51643–X

Phototypeset by Input Typesetting Ltd, London SW19 8DR
Printed in Great Britain by Anchor Brendon Ltd
Tiptree, Essex

To Conrad Pepler, o.p.
Warden of Spode House 1953–81

Contents

Preface

Recognising and responding to God is a challenge that faces the whole of mankind. It is a particular challenge to Western society which has both a Judaeo–Christian tradition and an unprecedented technological development. Men and women have to rediscover their sense of God in their work and their personal relationships, with Jesus Christ as the saving sacrament of the whole community.

This book is based on a model similar to my previous study, *Cycles of Affirmation*, which was published in 1975. It contained a number of articles on love, marriage and the single state which were designed to bring forth the Christian concept of relationship examined through contemporary psychology. Despite the disparate nature of the contents, the book has been and continues to be well received.

Soon afterwards an annual weekend conference was started at Spode House, with the general title, 'The Face of God in Contemporary Society'. These weekends have been continued for the last eight years and are attended by fifty to a hundred people. The theme of each conference is introduced by a speaker, followed by two papers from myself, and the weekend is rounded off by a study of the theme through the scriptures, which has been carried out, except for the first year, by Fr Fergus Kerr, o.p. There have been repeated requests to have some of the lectures of these weekends published and with the ever ready cooperation of my publishers this has been possible.

My aim has been to examine, in a limited and selected manner, the image of God in contemporary man, seeking perfection in personal relationships and in community through love and with what love implies in the context of both. The reader will find a variety of themes which aim to take contemporary subjects and examine their meaning in the light of psychology and Christianity. Love, authority, freedom, suffering, aggression and anxiety, amongst others, are each examined with the purpose of discovering how the topic can be understood in the overlap between psychology and Christianity. In each case there is a penetrating examination of the place that love plays in understanding the subject in depth, both psychologically and spiritually. Although we have edited these lectures, inevitably there is some repetition in order to retain the flow of the lecture.

Taken together, the contents are designed to illuminate contemporary themes of relevance in human relationships and to examine in detail how the insights of psychology inter-relate with a modern spirituality. I have tried to show throughout that an awareness of dynamic psychology is an invaluable tool in understanding not only the mechanisms of human behaviour but the depths of Christian spirituality.

Each theme is linked with particular aspects of Christ's life in mind and the book is written in anticipation of a more detailed psychological profile of Jesus Christ which is currently in preparation.

I have dedicated this book to Conrad Pepler, O.P. who was Warden at Spode House when these conferences started and who was always a tower of strength in making the practical arrangements. I want also to thank the audiences of the conferences who annually provided such a penetrating and inexhaustible source of constructive criticism. As ever, I want to thank my wife and members of my family for helping to get the material ready for publication.

September 1984

J. DOMINIAN

1

The Image of God in Contemporary Society

It is unlikely that anyone will disagree with the view that pluralism is the principal characteristic of contemporary society. When we look at our world today we see a multitude of nations whose economic structures vary from capitalism through socialism to communism, operated by political systems ranging from genuine democracy to various forms of tyrannical dictatorships within which populations struggle for existence, largely in poverty, some in affluence, and all caught in the confusion of the meaning of the ultimate. This ultimate is either in secular terms – the world and life around us conceived in terms of causes which are not basically absolutely necessary, rational or purposeful – or in religious terms in which the foundations of our being, our meaning, our value and purpose are related to a divine source.

I do not set out to prove the existence of God: that is the 'given', the basic assumption of all that follows. Furthermore this is the God of the Old and the New Testament, principally experienced and lived in the Roman Catholic tradition, but forming in fact the common denominator of all Christian belief. It is the image of God in contemporary society that is the subject of this book.

Theological Implications
What is the connection between the image of God and society? At the very beginning of the Old Testament in Genesis, we find the text:

> God said, Let us make man in our own image, in the likeness of ourselves, and let them be masters of the fish of the sea, the birds of heaven, the cattle, all the wild beasts

and all the reptiles that crawl upon the earth. God created man in the image of himself, in the image of God he created him, male and female he created them. (Genesis 1:26–7)

Later theology will argue what the words 'image' and 'likeness' mean, with a predominantly Catholic tradition running from Irenaeus onwards which will identify the image of God with reason and freedom of the personality, and likeness as the gift of supernatural communion with God, destroyed by sin and restored by Jesus Christ. This has come to be called the two-storey view of the universe, namely reason and freedom, unaided by faith, on which is superimposed the supernatural second storey of revealed truth and supernatural grace; in this way achieving the synthesis between Christianity and the Greek thought of Plato, Aristotle and Hellenistic philosophy. The reformers did not accept this interpretation of the words, image and likeness, and by implication the two-storey system. There was in fact for them only one storey, image and likeness being essentially the same thing, the privilege of the gift of standing in God's presence continuously as a responsible and moral person.

The way of interpreting image and likeness is intimately related to the impact of sin, original sin associated with the Fall. The Roman Catholic tradition maintains that sin removes the supernatural gifts and life of grace but leaves reason and freedom in man operating in his will; the Reformed position, interpreting man as a whole person, steady in responsible response before God, sees his capacity to respond as either totally corrupted or distorted and the will accordingly devastated.

Either interpretation paves the way for Jesus Christ who is the New Testament image of God. The Old Testament leaves man in a relationship with God, however distorted; the New Testament reveals Christ and his sacrifice as the source of restoration and reconciliation of the relationship of grace. How does the New Testament refer to the image?

Christ is described by Paul in the Epistle to the Colossians as: 'The image of the unseen God and the first-born of all creation, for in him were created all things in heaven and on earth: everything visible and everything invisible' (Colossians

1:15-16). Christ, the incarnate Son of God, is the image of that unseen God which we Christians see. Paul draws our attention in his Second Epistle to the Corinthians to the difference between the Old and the New dispensations. In the Old, Moses – and indeed the whole of Israel – had a veil over their face; that is to say their vision of God was limited by the law of the covenant; but now Christ has removed this veil from us and we can gaze and be illuminated directly by the Son of God. Paul, the Jew, writing in the first century A.D., appreciates most keenly the transition from the Old to the New dispensation and, referring to the Jews, says:

> Yes, even today, whenever Moses is being read, a veil never lifted, since Christ alone can remove it. It will not be removed until they turn to the Lord. Now this Lord is the Spirit and where the Spirit of the Lord is, there is freedom. And we, with our unveiled faces reflecting like mirrors the brightness of the Lord, all grown brighter and brighter as we are turned into that image that we reflect; this is the work of the Lord who is Spirit. (2 Corinthians 3:15–18)

God and man can now interact with an immediacy which Christ brought about. In John's Gospel we have the consummation of this interaction:

> Father, may they be one in us,
> As you are in me and I am in you,
> So that the world may believe it was you who sent me.
> I have given them the glory you gave to me,
> that they may be one as we are one.
> With me in them and you in me,
> may they be so completely one
> that the world will realise that it was you who sent me
> and that I have loved them as much as you loved me.
> (John 17: 22–3)

The Image as Love
The Old Testament reveals to us that we are created in the image of God, a God who creates and sustains the cosmos

and all that is within it. It is a world that, for some reason we do not fully understand, could not realise this image fully, through the intervention of sin, needing Christ the Son of God and the redeemer to restore the relationship between man and God and to show us the fullness of the image. But wherein lies this fullness? Clearly, as Aquinas tells us, all our descriptions of God use analogy, for by definition God is a mystery which cannot be fully grasped or described by us. Nevertheless one word provides the essential link for God's nature and activity, namely love. This creation, its sustenance and redemption are all explainable in terms of love.

In one of the briefest definitions of God, John in his First Epistle writes:

> God is love
> and anyone who lives in love lives in God,
> and God lives in him. (1 John 4:16)

God is love but in fact love operates through persons in the process of loving, the love of God manifests itself in his creation, its sustenance, redemption and in the relationship of the three persons of the Trinity; in his relationship to man, first directly and then through his Son, Jesus Christ. The key to love is through life, its sustenance, redemption in and through love of relationship, the relationship of the Trinity to man and that between man and man. We again refer to the First Epistle of John for clarification.

> God's love for us was revealed
> when God sent into the world his only Son
> so that we could have life through him. (1 John 4:9)

and again:

> My dear people,
> since God has loved us so much
> we too should love another.
> No one has ever seen God;
> But as long as we love one another God will live in us and
> his love will be complete in us. (1 John 4:11–12)

Finally we turn to Paul for the language of dynamic certainty of God's love.

> For I am certain of this: neither death nor life, no angel, no prince, nothing that exists, nothing still to come, not any power, or height or depth, nor any created thing can ever come between us and the love of God made visible in Christ Jesus our Lord. (Romans 8: 38–9)

In these days when faith is questioned from innumerable sources, Paul's certainty of the love of God, in and through Christ, comes through the ages as a clarion call challenging all Christians in all ages. But what is the nature of this love, where is it situated in any particular age, how is it to be recognised and realised?

The 'Image' as Relationship

If we return to the first reference in Genesis to the image, we find the words, 'God said, let us make man in our own image, in the likeness of ourselves.' Without entering into the exegesis of this line, its plural form is unmistakable, giving the early Fathers the possibility of seeing this text as a hint of the Trinity. Certainly in these circumstances the image is immediately placed in the context of plurality and relationship. Furthermore the image is followed immediately by the creation of man and woman in relationship to one another. The great Protestant theologian Karl Barth interprets the concept of image as existing in two relationships, the man-woman and man-God. Thus the nature of the love is essentially to be found in these two relationships but clearly the relationship of persons cannot be confined to heterosexuality, for love of neighbour, one of the principal teachings both of the Old and the New Testament, is not exclusive to the man-woman relationship.

Christ in fact summarises the meaning of love in relationship when he answers the question of the Pharisees regarding the greatest commandment of the law. Jesus replied:

> You must love the Lord your God with all your heart, with all your soul and with all your mind. This is the greatest

and the first commandment. The second resembles it. You must love your neighbour as yourself. On these two commandments hang the whole law and the Prophets also.' (Matthew 22: 36–40)

The Link between 'Image' and Community

All of us are familiar with the further unfolding of the concept of neighbour by the marvellous answer of Christ in the parable of the good Samaritan. None of us lives in isolation, and neighbour is any member of the community whom we are commanded to love. Indeed the symbol of the body of Christ as representing the community of Christians developed by Paul means indubitably that the image of God in man is always to be found in relationships of love, that between man and God extended between 'I' and 'thou' in community.

The Concept of 'Image' as Wholeness and Perfection

When we refer to an 'I' or a 'thou' we are referring to relationships between persons, and not persons and things, an 'I'–'it' encounter. Clearly it is the whole person then who reflects the image of God and is turned into it in and through Christ. This whole person, as Paul makes clear, includes all the elements of our humanity, body, mind and soul, and therefore involves not only the secular psychosomatic entity; the image of God requires a spiritual, psychosomatic wholeness. Finally this totality is required to be as perfect as our heavenly Father, a command – not a request – laid down by Christ.

Thus the image of God is a universal endowment of man by God, a gift of love, expressed in God's love of man and man's love of God and neighbour, first imperfectly and then fully, in and through Jesus Christ. This love is accomplished by the whole person who seeks perfection in the community. This is the background to the question already asked, namely how is this love expressed and where is it to be sanctified? The expression of this love has at times been concentrated on the potential of intellect and reason which emphasise man's contemplation of God in his glory, or a mystical union with him. The fact remains that man's perfection cannot possibly dismiss or ignore any part of his make-up and therefore any genuine and authentic progress towards perfection requires the fullest possible realisation of all man's potential and it is the orientation and availability of this potential to God and man that constitutes the meaning of perfection.

The Identification of this Love in Personal Relationships and Social Justice

Following this we reach the central point of the discussion, namely that in our contemporary world this love is identified in two principal situations, in personal relations and in social justice. Ideally we should be able to trace fully the meaning of love in personal relationship and social justice by examining man's progress and involvement, from childhood to death, in the family and in community. Religion is going through a phase when allegiance to formal structures and formal church attendance are under serious strain. God is in no way absent from consideration even in this so-called secular society, as the enormous interest in religious books, fringe religious practices and in Christ's humanity suggests. If, as St Augustine tells us, our hearts are made for God, then contemporary man – placed in the dilemma of repudiating the God of formal religion and practice – can always find God through prayer, however confused the address to God may be. Clearly what is suffering today is the encounter between man and God in the sacramental presence of Christ, as the Father's divinity is questioned and as the traditional forms of the sacraments make little sense even to the faithful. A fresh examination of the sacraments and the idea of the Church as the sacrament seems to me to be urgently called for but here personal relationships and social justice form the principal subjects through which the image of God in man is examined. The words 'image of God' are of course peculiarly suitable for Christians and the sacrament as the image of God has been fulfilled in the eternal Word that took flesh and encountered man face to face in the incarnation.

Matching Awareness

The recurrent examination of the image of God in man seems to me necessary for a particular reason which I have rarely seen expounded at any length. It is absolutely clear that, if man is to respond to God fully, then this can be done only when his humanity, his level of awareness and consciousness of what it means to be human, corresponds with what theology teaches about God's self-disclosure in the scriptures and tradition. I want to illustrate this essential need for matching human experiences with an adequate awareness of God, by making two points.

The contemporary apparent withdrawal from religion is the conclusion of at least three centuries of gradual emphasis on reason detached from God, and man's apparent self-sufficiency in the thought and philosophy of the three greats of the nineteenth and twentieth centuries, Darwin, Marx and Freud. So the present secular state is explained *ad nauseam* in these terms. Very little is said of Freud's criticism of religion, that it represents man's need of dependence on a power greater than himself, an extension of childhood needs of security, support and comfort given by the parents. What Freud's criticism suggests is far more than that religion is a universal neurosis. Implicit in the criticism is man's need to rely on an authority greater than himself. Both the Roman Catholic Church and, to a lesser extent, the Reformed Churches rely unconsciously on the authority of the structures and the ministers of the churches as a means of underpinning religion. Belief was facilitated because faith was mediated by human authority that supported the needs Freud speaks about, namely dependence, support, comfort and direction. Progressively, as the need for dependence on authority has diminished, so has the practice of faith. Hence only an accurate matching of man coming of age (a process, incidentally, which has been going far longer than the twentieth century) with the image of God, with whom he has a relationship, will prove a sufficient basis for faith. The thinking of Vatican II and of the other churches is progressing along these lines but the halting progress made indicates how much more theology is attached to the safety of the past, rather than risking the anxiety of rendering the man-God relationship meaningful. I am well aware that the word meaningful is grossly misused and justly attacked but it is also attacked by those who are simply frightened to move, for purely human reasons – such as the use of authority, whatever form it may take – to greater

8

reliance on the faith of Paul that nothing, but simply nothing, no discovery of man, can ever seriously threaten God's reality and his love.

The other point is that a whole generation of Roman Catholics grew up with an emphasis on saving their souls in a vertical relationship with God, hardly aware of salvation in and through community. The twentieth century is rightly obsessed with the salvation of the corporate in and through social justice. Only Christianity, with its powerful awareness of the dignity of every single person created in the image of God, can do justice to the individual and community concurrently. For this a massive new theology of social ethics is required to meet the arguments of the salvation of man and community and certainly to counter any secular salvation which emphasises community at the expense of the individual.

This is not to say that the Church has neglected this field. There are great social encyclicals since Leo XIII. There are however three serious weaknesses in these documents. First their principles are based on universals and propositions, on the pursuit of Truth through Justice, mediated by love and freedom. No one can quarrel with the principles but their application needs to meet local circumstances, such as currently applies, for example, in South America and Africa, in fact wherever man's dignity is under serious threat. There is a serious gap between the theory enunciated and the practical needs of a local situation. Secondly these encyclicals – as indeed the whole teaching of the Church – are weak on action and strong in theory when it comes to social justice. Thirdly they all tend to lean on the side of private property and the individual and against the State and collectivity. Whilst many will argue that this is absolutely correct, the fact remains that there are many parts of the world where this emphasis is grossly misused and private property remains the privilege of the few, supported by a tyrannical government.

In fact the Church has immense resources in its treasury to give the lead which balances the needs of the individual and the community; but this needs to be done in a way that meets different and differentiated conditions which are rapidly and constantly changing. A far more flexible theology is required which combines principles and practice, safe-guarding man from the anonymous community and the community from individuals and minorities wholly concerned with their own advantages and interests.

A sensitive awareness and matching of man's aspirations in different stages of development with God's image is the urgent need and reality of the world today.

The Image of God and Perfection

I want to conclude this section with the idea of perfection as related to the image of God. Professor Passmore's book, *The Perfectibility of Man*, and David Cairn's *The Image of God*, which are the background texts of my theme, have summarised the secular and religious human attempts to attain perfection. The arguments between the Roman Catholic Church and the Reformers regarding man's ability to attain and contribute to his perfection are well known. The uniqueness of Christianity is that it is a religion based on a relationship with a God, who is a person and our Father, a relationship affected by sin, but with whom we have a personal encounter in and through Jesus Christ, mediated by love through the Spirit. Both the Old and the New Testament refer continuously to God's glory revealed in his revelation and in the crown of the logos, Jesus Christ. John's Gospel – as indeed the Pauline epistles – stress this glory of Jesus as reflecting the unseen God. John writes, 'The Word was made flesh, he lived among us, and we saw his glory, the glory that is his as the only Son of the Father, full of grace and truth' (John 1:14).

It is natural then to see the concept of perfection primarily in terms of man's progress towards understanding the mystery and glory of God and living this in his moral and spiritual life. Progress has been equated with the spiritual and moral dimension, with human progress considered as secondary. This is a view of man which is incomplete. The image of God in man involves the whole person – body, mind, soul – that relates to God, in and through personal relationship and the life of the community which he occupies. The glory of God in man corresponds to man as a historical person, reflecting as fully as possible his full potential in relationship to other persons and to the cosmos he inhabits. Hence contemporary humanism is no threat to Christianity when it is recognised that God's glory and image is constantly being responded to by our ever deepening and enlarging humanity, conscious of the Kingdom preached and proclaimed by Jesus Christ. God's gift to man is life, total life to be lived in relationships of love with God and man, always acknowledging that the source of life and love is God to whom ultimately all life is to be reconciled in the fullness of eschatological being. The belief of Christianity is that the image of God, with its implicit perfection, is a gift that man is capable of realising in this world and in the eschatological reality of the next without end.

2

Personal Relationships

The image of God in personal relationships is basically a reflection of the person interacting as an individual in one-to-one relationships, largely the concern of psychology and psychiatry; and the person as a member of a group, the family, work unit and the larger units of society, the area of sociology. Useful as it is to delineate these two disciplines for purposes of research and information gathering, ultimately it is the personal resources of the individual that govern the quality of relationship in singular or group situations. Accordingly the starting point will be the individual, involving an examination of love in terms of his resources, how these develop and in what manner their availability reflects the expression of love.

The Essence of Person
In this context I shall use the brief definition I made in *Proposals for a New Sexual Ethic,* namely, that a person is a psychosomatic unity who, from the time of conception onwards, realises his/her physical, intellectual, psychological (affective and cognitive perspectives) and spiritual dimensions within the particular socio-economic matrix of society. The psychological key to being a person is the dynamic concept of wholeness, that is to say, having access in a balanced form to all one's dimensions, both conscious and unconscious; and growth, a continuous process which allows the realisation of one's potential.

Following from this description, we can see that the first task of every person is to acquire possession of themselves and to do so in a manner which is positive, in other words to be aware of our various characteristics, to recognise them

12

as our own and to invest them with a sense of goodness. To be and to feel good in being oneself is the key to self-love and self-love is the key to all personal loving, for unless we recognise our resources and feel these are good we have nothing to donate to others, nor have we the means of receiving the love of others because there is no part of ourselves that is recognised or feels good enough to be appreciated. Psychology has helped us to understand in human terms the meaning of the sentence in the first Epistle of St John: 'We are to love, then, because he loved us first' (1 John 4:19). Our first experience of love is from our parents and this will now be examined in detail.

THE PSYCHOLOGICAL CRITERIA OF LOVE

Ownership and Autonomy

All of us are aware of the child's gradual growth, physically, intellectually and psychologically. This is a journey from absolute oneness and dependence, a total fusion of child and mother, through a gradual separation of some two decades, at the end of which we should ideally recognise and feel that our bodies, minds and feelings belong to us, are ours for donation to others and that they are invested with a feeling of worth.

The ability to own, possess or have full access to these dimensions depends on the one hand on the endowment of the child and on the other on the attitude and handling of parents, who see themselves merely as temporary custodians of the life of their child, in no way to be possessed or retained for their own ends but as guardians of a precious responsibility, the deliverance of a whole and intact person with the capacity to recognise and feel that they possess themselves fully and are free, autonomous, self-governing persons.

Psychiatry has recognised that no freedom is as precious as that of fully possessing ourselves, having access to as much of ourselves as possible, for it is from this ownership that the whole basis of being is safeguarded. All over the world clinicians see millions of people who, in their twenties, thirties, forties, fifties and even later, are confused about their identity, not knowing who and what they are; frightened to use their bodies, still damaged by parental fears of their delicate nature, or to enjoy their sexuality because of parental attitudes, to feel free to think and use their own thoughts, which appear to usurp the right of parents to be the sole origins of thought and initiative; able to experience little else except the anxiety of incompetence because their bodies, minds and feelings were invested with a minimum capacity to exist on their own, independent of parental support, guidance and approval.

Naturally it takes the whole of our lives to explore the richness of what we own, of what we are, but the first necessary criterion for this exploration is to feel free to experience that which belongs to us as our own.

The Quality of Ownership

(a) Trust. It is not enough for our parents to facilitate the ever growing movement towards independence which the growing child needs. The qualities with which we experience the various parts of ourselves are just as vital and form another characteristic of the love of self.

The basic quality which is essential to love of self is trust. Our bodies, minds and emotions must feel trustworthy, a characteristic gradually achieved in continuous interaction between ourselves as children and our parents.

Thus, because our parents helped us to feel safe in our bodies, our bodies feel safe and reliable to be used as energy machines, and as the means of expressing and receiving love in intimate encounters. All our first experiences of safety and satisfaction were bodily mediated in the arms of our mother and father. If our bodies feel safe and reliable, they become a language of transmitting love to others as they transmit signals of recognition, welcome and security through physical contact and finally a return to total oneness through sexual intercourse. Similarly, because our minds have been invested with the sense of reliability and credibility, we can turn to their resources to evaluate meaning and order in the world and to enrich it with the beauty of creative art in words, music, painting, sculpture and art in general. It is reliable thought and its transmission that creates civilisation. Finally because our emotions and instinctual characteristics are recognised and become reliable we are able to survive physical dangers, communicate and be informed of emotional distress, and avoid the isolation of emotions and instincts from the wholeness of our person. The integration of aggression and sexuality protects us from a rampage which fragments our personality or destroys and exploits others through the uncontrolled eruption of impulses.

(b) Initiative. Our parents are primarily responsible for helping us gradually to acquire possession of ourselves, to feel that the constituent parts of our self are trustworthy so that we can experience ourselves as reliable persons and also encourage us to be able to engage the reliable resources we have acquired in both active and reflective processes. The ability to use our bodies with initiative means that we are capable of moving physically towards others in order to interact and are not afraid of personal and social contact as the thousands of men and women who suffer from social phobias are. It also means that we can pursue with our bodies exploration, creativity and athletic prowess. But initiative is not always an active process, it has also the ability to receive sensitively the signals others transmit and respond accurately to anxiety, fear, danger, pain and joy. Our minds are constantly called upon to take the initiative with fresh thought and reflective response to the thought of others. Our emotions are equally called upon to initiate and express fear, pain, anger, sexuality and pleasure and to register sensitively, accurately and reciprocally the emotions of others.

(c) Competence. Part of our lack of initiative results from the fear of failure. An essential part of being loved by our parents and teachers is to facilitate in us the awareness that what appears initially an unfathomable gap between their knowledge and competence and ours is transformed gradually to one of equality of knowledge and competence and perhaps ultimately to the recognition that the emerging adult is better endowed than those responsible for their development.

Since, however, even with the most enabling and facilitating parents, we have to face the reality of our physical, intellectual and emotional limitations, what is the ultimate quality which we need to possess that gives us an enduring sense of value, despite our obvious shortcomings in our talents and our repeated partial or complete failures?

Personal Significance

In the course of our gradual separation, growth of ownership of self, awareness of our reliability, initiative and competence and all the opposite qualities of undue dependence, self-doubt, fear of initiative and incompetence, there is a continuous interaction between ourselves as children and our parents, in which we acquire a personal awareness of significance. We arrive at the ultimate of self-love, if we grow up, with whatever resources we possess, conscious that we are unconditionally accepted, not because of our resources but because we exist. We feel wanted, accepted and appreciated unconditionally because we are, in existential terms, an 'I'.

Personal Wounds and Social Limitations

Needless to say no constitution is endowed genetically with perfection and no parents or teachers are so perfect in their facilitation that anyone of us emerges from our childhood without some wounds. The extent and intensity of these influence our subsequent relationships a great deal, and here we come to one of the principal features of the image of God in personal relationships in our age. This is an age conscious as never before of the balance between integrity and wholeness on the one hand and injury and fragmentation on the other in the human personality. The recognition of these characteristics in depth is one of the unique phenomena of our age, unfolding the image of God in man to an extent never before appreciated or realised in populations at large. Furthermore this awareness has both influenced and brought about a change in personal relationships in which expectancy that the depths of the personality will be recognised and responded to has altered the character of all personal relationships of intimacy, from friendship to the exclusive and personal one-to-one relationship of marriage. The growing psychological awareness needs a social response, in this case a certain freedom from material needs of survival such as food, disease and poverty, because – in the presence of the latter – a penetrating psychological awareness has to yield to the priorities of physical survival. Only when a society has a certain degree of freedom from the threat of physical extinction can it respond fully to the awareness of the discoveries of the psychological sciences. This combination of material affluence and psychological awareness is to be found in approximately a third of the world today and it is here that the accent of the image of God in man must be placed on love realised through personal relationships.

In writing this I am perfectly conscious that, although psychological knowledge can go on advancing at a rapid rate, social conditions are far more vulnerable and the dangers of poverty are constantly threatening, if not the whole, at least substantial parts of Western society. If however the world progresses towards an equalisation of living standards, then our advanced knowledge of psychology in the West and its relevance to personal relationships will become widespread throughout the world in the next hundred years.

First Intimate Experience and Love
Thus we emerge from our first intimate experience in life, that between ourselves and our parents, with all the essentials of love already established. The first two decades of life should ideally give us all the essential characteristics of love of self and prepare us in outline for love of neighbour.

Sustaining
Sustaining has two dimensions, material and emotional. Clearly the responsibility we have for the physical well-being of our neighbour varies according to the commitment and responsibility we have assumed for them and will vary between the married and non-married. But sustaining has also an emotional dimension whose principal feature is the offering of ourselves in a sensitive response to the other, the 'thou', in a manner which sustains their significance by feeling uncritically recognised, wanted and appreciated. In other words, there is a basic difference between loving, in which we respond to another as a person to whom we make ourselves available in affirming their significance unconditionally, and a contractual relationship in which our availability is based on an equal exchange. We do something for them in return

for what they do for us. Loving sustaining is not remotely utilitarian in character but continues the basic intimate exchange of childhood affirmation of the worth of another, now no longer parent affirming child but one grown-up affirming another grown-up. Sustaining personal significance in another, particularly through periods of depression, desolation and isolation, is a vital part of our loving.

Our capacity to do this is directly related to our own resources of love of self, our own ability to be sensitively aware of the needs of another, to overcome the fact that for long periods we may have to sustain without an equal and reciprocal support from them as their resources are at a low ebb. This depends on reliable resources within ourselves that do not need to be immediately replenished in order to sustain another and that can accept longish periods of little return from those we support. It hardly needs mentioning that, if our resources are pretty limited or our love of self is minimal, then how much of ourselves we can donate in a sustained effort is likely to be limited too and become easily overwhelmed by frustration, disappointment and lack of visible success. We can easily identify the poor lover whose exuberance for a cause, be it the needs of another person or persons, is sustained only if there is quick and visible success, in the absence of which the person or persons are blamed for being lazy, not trying enough and not helping themselves enough.

Healing

As already mentioned, the wounds we bring to our second intimate relationship in adult life are the result of our constitutional make-up, physical disabilities or psychological ones, such as an excessive tendency to mood-swings of depression or mania, excessive anxiety (with or without psychosomatic manifestations), phobias, obsession traits or other handicaps; or of the way the environment, principally our parents, treated us, or more correctly how our constitutional make-up interacted with the way our parents behaved towards us. I add this because otherwise it appears that parents bear the sole responsibility for anything that goes wrong. This is not true; parents offer themselves but what the child registers depends on its own capacities. However, if we go beyond these technicalities many people emerge from childhood with small or powerful erosions in their capacity to feel secure or to trust others, deprived of affection or of the feeling of significance, lacking in self-esteem or confidence, unable to register love because they feel basically unlovable, unable to love back because they feel they are empty or – even worse – they experience a combination of guilt and badness so that what they have to offer is not worth much.

Our modern era of psychological healing was introduced by Freud and has subsequently been enlarged by the behaviourist school. From their theories what emerges is this. Provided we have a sufficiently intimate and secure relationship with another person we can expose our wounds, which means that we have to feel the pain of our isolation, helplessness, worthlessness and rejection and communicate it. If the 'other' is sensitive enough to respond (and this is of course the risk we take, namely to expose our pain and be ignored or dismissed in the process, which simply magnifies the wound), then healing can take place. The 'other' can provide us in this second round of intimate relationships with the ingredients of recognition, acceptance and appreciation, which goes a long way to help us to unlearn our previous experience and substitute an appropriate one.

The possibility of healing in intimate relationships is one of the most precious characteristics which the psychological sciences have given to us and we are just at the beginning of realising the magnitude of the possibilities involved. In fact we are temporarily experiencing the very opposite. People have reached the stage of exposing their wounds to each other well in advance of our general understanding of how to respond and the failure to respond accurately has disseminated a widespread feeling of pessimism, desolation, cynicism and the trend of moving from person to person seeking relentlessly the healing we desire, instead of persisting in one relationship. The rate of marital breakdown is one indication of this.

Growth
It is difficult to understand what we mean by growth when we go beyond absolute physical and intellectual development,

19

both of which are completed in the second half of the second decade. Growth beyond that is concerned with the transformation of physical resources into the competent and efficient excellence of the athlete or the creative use of our hands. The exploration of the intellectual resources leads ultimately to greater acquisition of truth and wisdom and the growth of feelings and emotions leads to a balance in which sensitive awareness is greater than apathy and insensitivity, patience is greater than impatience, tolerance greater than frustration and impulsiveness, affirmation greater than invalidation, reconciliation greater than conflict and aggression. This growth is seen in better utilisation of recognised potential but it also involves the development of latent resources. Most of us need a loving 'other' to recognise what is hidden within us, to encourage us with our hesitant experiments of new discoveries, to sustain and confirm our efforts to enlarge our potential and to enlarge it as a whole, so that if we are strong in reason we do not neglect our feelings and emotions, and if we are good at communicating the latter we bring order and discipline into our thinking, and if we are good at both we do not neglect the potential of our body. In particular however wholeness requires both reason and feelings and the exaltation of one at the expense of the other has been a great error of much traditional Roman Catholic theology. In order to facilitate the growth of the 'other', our own life must be sufficiently free of envy or jealousy not to feel threatened by the advancement of our neighbour. Naturally if we feel their advance spells out our demise, then, far from promoting their growth, we will do all we can consciously and unconsciously to keep them at our level and, if possible, undermine them since their diminution will bolster up our image. Many an intimate relationship lives exactly on this principle of destructive competition which is the very opposite of love promoting growth.

Sustaining, healing and growth are the principal marks of loving our neighbour which in turn requires love of self as its basis. All loving of neighbour ultimately succeeds to the extent of our availability and this in turn depends on the love of self. For thousands of years love of neighbour has been seen in the broad terms of seeking their good and that good has only too often been seen in terms of material needs and the freedom of the person. In Western societies loving, although still concerned, as it will indeed always continue to be concerned, with material needs, has penetrated the next layer of being in terms of healing and growth.

To conclude with a famous passage from the Epistle to the Philippians:

> If our life in Christ means anything to you, if love can persuade at all, or the Spirit that we have in common. . . That is one thing which would make me completely happy. There must be no competition among you, no conceit, but everybody is to be self-effacing. Always consider the other person to be better than yourself, so that nobody thinks of his own interest first but everybody thinks of other people's interests instead. In your minds you must be the same as Christ Jesus. His state was divine, yet he did not cling to his equality with God but emptied himself to assume the condition of a slave, and became as men are. (Philippians 2:1–7)

Here is a classical passage interpreted repeatedly as a model of humility and self-effacing. What is completely ignored repeatedly by those who confine their ethical commentary to self-diminution is the fact that Christ could not have emptied himself unless he was first full and, at the end of the Epistle to the Colossians, after emphasising the magnitude of the transformation for those who have taken on the new life of Christ, this is what Paul has to say:

> You have stripped off your old behaviour with your old self, and you have put on a new self which will progress towards true knowledge the more it is renewed in the image of its creator; and in that image there is no room for the distinction between Greek and Jew, between the circumcised or the uncircumcised, or between barbarian and scythian, slave and free man. There is only Christ: he is everything and he is in everything. (Colossians 3:9–11)

Christ is everything and only the fullness of everything can empty himself fully. Likewise with each one of us we can only make ourselves fully available to others and donate our whole self, if that self is first affirmed and confirmed in fullness of self-acceptance as Christ is in and through the Father. As Christ was the image of the unseen God, so man, created in the image of God, reflects it in and through Christ, a reflection that can only do justice to the image the greater is the love which is in all of us first, in order to be available to others.

3

Authority and Integrity I

The Meaning of Authority
Most of us think of authority as a characteristic of those
people who possess the legitimate right to our obedience and
compliance. We are heavily conditioned to this interpretation
because our earliest experiences were those of obeying our
parents, teachers and generally all those who were bigger,
stronger and wiser than we were.

This emotional sense of authority, which is linked with a
family structure in which parents – but particularly the father
– had power over the members of the household, has
continued into the life of the Church. The Church has been
experienced as a hierarchical institution with authority vested
in the hands of the pope, bishop, priest, all male figures called
Fathers, who until very recently directed the laity. Life inside
the Church has been greatly preoccupied with this theme.
Since Vatican II, concepts such as collegiality, delegation of
authority and the role of the laity have been under constant
discussion. In an age which is challenging all authority, this
turmoil inside the Church is to be expected.

Implicit in the concept of authority is the presence of power
and the ability of enforcement. There are various figures of
authority in society all of whom have power given to them
from different sources. Parents, teachers, doctors, the police,
judges, members of parliament, wield different powers. These
include the use of physical force, the protection of the law,
the wisdom and experience of the individual or the ability to
persuade, a charismatic quality.

I suppose at all times in the history of man human beings
have looked for the ideal, which is the combination of
appointed authority with personal resources that match and

complement the office. Certainly in our times the power of an authority figure is probed relentlessly and any incongruity between status and talents is remorselessly exposed in free societies.

When it comes to the authority of God we can only act on the basis that person and authority are fused in a quality of ideal perfection in which the power of the divine lies in its integrity.

The *Shorter Oxford English Dictionary* describes the word integrity as wholeness, lack of corruption, perfect condition, sinlessness, uprightness and sincerity.

Clearly then the impact of Jesus Christ, the incarnate Word, must have been largely mediated in the authority which he manifested in his life which reflects his integrity.

In this chapter an examination will be made of authority in terms of integrity in general.

The Authority of Jesus

There is little doubt that Jesus conveyed an impression of authority. We find in the Gospel of St Matthew the amazement of the crowds when they listened to him: 'Jesus had now finished what he wanted to say; his teaching made a deep impression on the people, because he taught them with authority, and not like their own scribes' (Matthew 7:28–9).

The authorities were in fact aware that he had a convincing manner and furthermore he seemed both to affirm and challenge the law and they in turn kept questioning him and trying to trap him. Again in Matthew we find the chief priests and the elders of the people coming to him and asking: 'What authority have you for acting like this? And who gave you this authority?' (Matthew 21:23). His authority is in fact portrayed in his behaviour, acts and teaching which authenticates the majestic conclusion of St Matthew's Gospel:

All authority in heaven and in earth has been given to me. Go, therefore, make disciples of all the nations; baptise them in the name of the Father and of the Son and of the Holy Spirit, and teach them to observe all the commands I gave you. And know that I am with you always: yes, to the end of time. (Matthew 28:18–20)

The image of God is unmistakably present in the authority of Jesus Christ. We see the Father in the Son and indeed the apostles, the crowds, the believers must have been greatly influenced in their response to Jesus by their natural reaction that they were in the presence of someone whose authority largely depended on his integrity. This integrity ultimately penetrated his physical, intellectual, social, psychological and spiritual dimensions. In whatever manner he was tested, the evidence of the scriptures supports the presence of a person who impressed by the integrity of his life. In so far as we are baptised in Jesus Christ, the image of God is imprinted in all of us. We are all invited to journey in integrity but the problem is to identify what we mean by it.

Possession of Self
One of the first characteristics of integrity is the freedom to be. From the first moment of our conception we have the challenge to grow and function effectively, to live our life fully and to the best of our ability. This ability depends on our healthy development, the realisation of our potential, but above all on the possession of ourselves.

In the course of growing up we continuously use our ever-expanding functions. We use our bodies and minds, shaped by our feelings and the sense of the spiritual. But there are two elements which have to be negotiated. The first is the fact that for a major part of our first two decades we are under the influence of our parents, relatives and teachers. They formulate our ideas, values, opinions, attitudes and, to a considerable extent, we reflect these in our own life.

There needs to be not only a physical but also a social, intellectual and emotional separation between ourselves and those in authority over us. In the process of this separation we begin to evaluate the given and gradually make our own choices. This is a gradual process of possessing ourselves which continues throughout our life. It is a process through which we differentiate what truly belongs to ourselves from what is being blindly followed. There is a critical separation between the choices we make on the basis of our own evaluation in life and the values which have been invested in us by others. This does not mean that we have to reject all that is received but it does mean that, if retained, it has to be gradually moulded by our own priorities and of course may need radically changing.

This process of separation is an essential part of possessing ourselves and it means that our commitment to others must not be based on fear or emotional dependence. We are not truly in possession of ourselves if we comply with the wishes of others because we are afraid of the consequences of not doing so.

There is a complication here. It is possible to divest ourselves of external influences to the extent that they are conscious but be influenced by unconscious ones. We need others to help us with our unconscious but occasionally we are confronted by it in our dreams, slips of the tongue or emotional behaviour which we do not comprehend.

As mentioned before the conscious possession of our bodies, minds and feelings is in turn of little use if we do not feel that what we possess is good. There are many people who are hindered by feelings of unworthiness, lack of self-esteem and confidence which leads to behaviour that is tentative, suggestive and unsure. Such behaviour, when challenged, tends to retract hastily because it does not spring from a conviction that is served by the whole infrastructure of the person.

The gradual divesting of ourselves of external influences, the discovery of our unique qualities and the ability to express freely what we believe is good and right, form the background of integrity.

We see all these steps in the life of our Lord. Whatever the nature of the account of the episode at the Temple, when Jesus was twelve, it shows an early separation between himself and his parents. He asks his parents, 'Why were you looking for me? Did you not know that I must be busy with my Father's affairs?' (Luke 2:49). The process of separation had already begun and, although he was to spend many years with his earthly parents, there is little doubt that all the time he was delineating himself from the immediate influences of his environment. At a later stage, when he was preaching and a message was given to him that his family were asking for him outside, he replied, 'Who are my mother and my brothers?' And looking around at them sitting in a circle

26

about him, he said: 'Here are my mother and my brothers. Anyone who does the will of God, that person is my brother and sister and mother' (Mark 3:33–5).

Our Lord had gradually separated himself from his immediate family and developed an identity which was unequivocally at the service of his father. Furthermore he had no doubt who he was in this state of separateness from his immediate surroundings. John is the evangelist who portrays this identity most clearly:

Then as Jesus taught in the Temple he cried out:

'Yes, you know me and you know where I came from,
Yet I have not come of myself:
No, there is one who sent me and I really care for him,
and you do not know him,
but I know him because I have come from him
and it was he who sent me.' (John 7:28–9)

Not only does he know who he is but he knows that his person is loved and that his father wants him freely to offer his life for us:

The father loves me,
because I lay down my life in order to take it up again.
No one takes it from me;
I lay it down of my own free will
and as it is in my power to lay it down,
so it is in my power to take it up again. (John 10:17–18)

Here we have an example of the forging of separateness of self which is set clearly on a course chosen by a self who possesses himself completely and feels that what he has to offer – his life, no less – is an acceptable gift to God the Father. A secure possession of a separate self which feels it can be donated is a supreme example of loving availability. These are the foundations of identity. At least these are the intentions of our Lord and we have to see what obstacles he and we have to overcome.

Inner Person

Each one of us has to negotiate a private life, in which we recognise our inner feelings, opinions and attitudes and relate intimately to those close to us, and a public life. Psychologists talk about self and identity as representatives of this private life and sociologists of the role we occupy in our public life in relation to others. The demands made on us in the two spheres of acting are different and an important test of our integrity is the presence of a continuity between our private and public life, between our external proclamation and our convictions and the reality of our private life. The confessional and the psychiatrist's consulting room have become the repositories of the gap between the inner and the outer, and conscience bears the burdens between the proclaimed and the realised.

There is no doubt, however, about the importance of the inner world. It is the heart with its feelings and emotions that motivates so much of our life. This much is clear in the teaching of Jesus. He was confronted with the particular situation of his time which the Pharisees and scribes maintained, namely the importance of the observance of the minutest detail of the law. External observance was of the greatest importance in preserving the right and the good. Jesus does not destroy this law of external requirements but he emphasises the importance of the inner life. In a powerful passage in Matthew, Jesus has to drive the point home in his preaching and even with his apostles.

He called the people to him and said, 'Listen and understand. What goes into the mouth does not make a man unclean; it is what comes out of that mouth that makes him unclean.'

Then the disciples came to him and said, 'Do you know that the Pharisees were shocked when they heard what you said?' He replied: 'Any plant my heavenly Father has not planted will be pulled up by the roots. Leave them alone. They are blind men; and if one blind man leads another, both will fall into a pit.'

At this Peter said to him, 'Explain the parable for us.' Jesus replied: 'Do even you not yet understand? Can you not see that whatever goes into the mouth passes through the stomach and is discharged into the sewer. But the things that come out of the mouth come from the heart, and it is these that make a man unclean. For from the heart come evil intentions: murder, adultery, fornication, theft, perjury, slander. These are the things that make a man unclean. But to eat with unwashed hands does not make a man unclean.' (Matthew 15:10–20)

This exchange between Jesus and the disciples has important implications for us today. Roman Catholics were used to an authoritative teaching which emphasised minute details of personal conduct. We remember the laws of fasting and abstinence, fasting before communion and a host of other rules. One of the features of Vatican II is the reasserting of the inner life in terms of the supreme importance of conscience. There has been a continuous debate in the Church between those who want to return to an emphasis of instructions and those who want to assert the freedom of conscience. Clearly we cannot make decisions in a vacuum and there would be a serious loss if the Church suddenly abandoned its teaching role. On the other hand, making decisions requires maturity, evaluation, judgment and effort, and at all times men and women are looking for short cuts to the business of living and particularly to the achievement of goodness. The debate in the life of our Lord continues today but neither then nor now is there any doubt where the seat of integrity is situated. It lies in our inner world where feelings and emotions play such a vital role and the action of the will is strongly influenced by these.

The Outer Person
But in everyday life it is not this inner world which is on view. In public life we have to carry out the functions which our job requires and the duties of the social obligations to which we commit ourselves. There are great pressures in public life to conform, to look and behave according to social expectations, and a great strain is placed on integrity in the course of having to act according to our proclaimed intentions. It is relatively easy to say what should be done, to

pretend in the course of short-lived periods of work and public duties, and in fact to act quite differently when we are out of the public gaze or public scrutiny.

The tests of integrity in public life challenge the dimensions of truth, honesty and justice. People say one thing and believe or do something else. They subscribe to honesty and do their best to cheat. They want justice for themselves but are indifferent to the claims of others.

The Gospel of John devotes much of its theology to Jesus representing the truth. John brilliantly shows that the truth is a combination of all that contributes to being in the inner and outer, the conscious and the unconscious, the uttered and the withheld, the ideal and the reality, the becoming and the arrived. All this is summed up as the evangelist puts into the mouth of our Lord the words:

> I am the way, the Truth and the Life:
> No one can come to the Father
> except through me.
> If you know me, you know my Father too.
> From this moment you know him and have seen him.
> (John 14:6–7)

Not only is Jesus the total manifestation of the divine but also our living model. When we are looking for the image of God, we find the invisible in the visible, in Christ's life.

Christ lived in the world but declared unequivocally that neither he nor those who follow him belong to the world. Between them the world and the flesh are two great impediments to integrity.

The World

Once again the Gospel of John shows clearly that, whilst our life is in the world – or in Teilhard de Chardin's term we live in a divine milieu – we are not of the world, we have to avoid being overwhelmed or crushed by the world.

> I, the light, have come into the world
> so that whoever believes in me
> need not stay in the dark any more.

If anyone hears my words and does not keep them
                                              faithfully,
it is not I who shall condemn him,
since I have come not to condemn the world
but to save the world. (John 12:46–7)

But the world is capable of choking the truth and destroying our integrity.

There have always been men and women who are so sensitive to this danger that they have chosen to flee from the world and live an alternative life in the desert, in a community, in religious life, in the privacy of an inner life dedicated to God. But in fact nobody can detach themselves completely from the world and the challenge is to live in the world and yet at the same time have a life in which love, the essence of the kingdom of God, predominates over the supreme values of the world.

The errors we have to guard against are rampant in our secular society. Perhaps its chief trap is that this world and the visible are the beginnings and conclusions of life. In these circumstances it makes more sense than ever to seek power in all its forms, material gain and the pursuit of pleasure. Against power Christ puts service of God. He contrasts the perishable uncertainty of material treasure with the enduring peace of love. Sacrifice is interposed between pleasure and joy. The world makes constant demands on us, drawing our energy by compelling us to focus on the struggle of survival. Survival is intimately linked with quantity, with amount of food, money, property and power, and is not concerned with quality. The kingdom that Christ preached is a world where quality stands predominant. It is a kingdom where happiness is related to gentleness, righteousness, mercy, purity, peace and openness to the spirit.

The Flesh
When quantity is discussed, the instinctual pleasures of the flesh, particularly the lust of food and sex, present themselves immediately. The sins of the flesh have been notoriously related to sex and here indeed there appears to exist an insatiable appetite of pleasure which has as its objective sheer

31

quantity. It is a very good example to illustrate another aspect of integrity, namely the presence of the partial, the incomplete. Against quantity has to be placed quality and against the partial has to be placed the whole. Nothing exemplifies the corrosive nature of the partial more than the use of sex.

The full use of human sexuality requires the fusion of the personal and the instinctual in a service to life, always the life of the person loved and occasionally new life. When sex is used only instinctively there is a separation between body and person and the partial is glorified. In the past we thought that the heart of purity consisted in the avoidance of the flesh. We now realise more fully that it is not the avoidance of the flesh that is commended but the integrity of the whole person. This integrity, which requires constant effort and sacrifice to love, transforms the sexual experience from the limitations of pleasure alone to the joy of inter-personal communion of whole persons. Such communion is so challenging that we can only interpret it with one person and it requires the qualities of continuity and reliability as the marks of faithfulness.

But the seduction of the flesh is not to be found in sexuality alone. There are other dangers when we avoid loving through tiredness, all the limitations of shyness, anxiety and fear which make us undemonstrative of affection and lacking in appreciation. The absence of physical demonstrations of affection is a loss, the presence of aggression is a risk that leads us to active damage and even killing of another.

The body is a remarkable organism for expressing love. It is also an awful means of displaying and producing destruction. When it is encouraged to be a machine without a heart, then it can press buttons, manipulate knobs and push handles which can cause havoc and destruction by remote control. In this way it is possible to transform the body into a thing which can be treated as expendable.

The Whole

Reference has been made to the need to trust sexuality as an expression of the whole person and perhaps there is nothing which denotes wholeness more than the movement of the integrated, of the whole, in relation to self and others. The use of body, mind, emotions and spirit as a totality is the constant challenge for all of us. Psychological studies have displayed to the full the limitations of various dichotomies. The person who uses his intellect but is without feelings is unlikely to empathise with others. The feeling person who cannot evaluate is likely to misjudge and misplace their feelings. The person who lives predominantly through his instincts has always been criticised for failing to do justice to reason and to the will.

We are constantly pulled apart and in various directions by our constituent parts and much of the damage to our humanity is caused when parts of men are idealised or elevated at the expense of others. The poor man of reason, of physical powers, of emotional moment, of intent badly executed, of ideals separated from reality is always incomplete. What is the common factor that avoids lack of excess? The Greeks praised the perfection of the mean, the Romans the order of law and the Judaeo–Christian tradition elevated the concept of love as the supreme value.

Love
I started this chapter with the emphasis on the gradual acquisition of the sense of ourselves through the possession of our bodies, minds, feelings and the spiritual as positive characteristics with which we live. These characteristics have a different priority in the unfolding of our life but they all form an integrated whole which constitutes the self. The possession of self which feels good has a purpose and that is to relate to life in the form of things, ideas and, above all, others. Its ultimate consummation is union through relationships of love and this union is marked by donation of self or availability. The mark of integrity is to be capable of experiencing reliably a whole sense of ourselves which is available to others and to God, in and through love. This love means a constant emptying of ourselves to others, to our spouses, children, relations, friends, colleagues and the world at large. The greater the command of ourselves, the greater is the sense of our availability. But what we have to offer has to be the expression of our whole self. So often we love

33

incompletely because we offer parts of ourselves which are in turn distorted by our lack of freedom, biases and prejudices, by ignorance, anxieties and fears.

Love and wholeness are seen repeatedly in the actions of Jesus. He took pity on the sick, the poor, the needy, the deprived and made his love known by repairing their damage. But the repairing was not only directed at the manifest problem. He linked healing with faith and forgiveness of sins, in other words with the arrival of wholeness.

But his most unique availability was in the Eucharist and the cross, the total emptying of himself out of love for our sake. His final act of love required the offering of a total and intact self to his Father. The integrity of his being was perfect and in it we find the conjunction of life and love and by implication the overthrow of death and the limitations of love. His ultimate authority was to be found in the triumph of life, death and resurrection.

Our authority is also to be found in our integrity which in turn lives in and shares that of Christ. Paul describes this in various passages and summarises the point thus: 'I have been crucified with Christ and I live now not with my own life but with the life of Christ who lives in me' (Galatians 2:20).

4

Authority and Integrity II

In the previous chapter I drew attention to the concept of authority as integrity and explained this integrity largely in the public life of the individual. There is also a whole private dimension of integrity which applies to personal relationships.

Formation of Relationship

The whole of Christianity is based on the incarnation, which in turn is a reflection of the relationship between Christ and his Father. Thus the establishment and maintenance of relationship lies at the very centre of being. The formation of human relationship has been examined extensively psychologically and what follows is a brief résumé of this.

The infant arrives in this world without any social or psychological personal relationships but it soon establishes these. During the course of the first year of life a strong attachment is formed with its mother or other close figures who nurture it. This attachment is strongly based on physical characteristics. The baby forms a close bond with its mother by recognising and responding to her physical appearance, voice, touch and smell. This intimacy is at first mediated through physical proximity. The child is held, cuddled, caressed, played with and recognises the mother and the immediate world around as a place of safety. It takes about three years to learn how to separate physically from her and stay for a few hours in the morning in a play group. Another two years will pass before the young child can stay away from mother for the whole day. Thus physical proximity and actual closeness form the infrastructure of human relationship.

Gradually however this physical intimacy is replaced for the major part of time by separateness and autonomy. The emerging person learns to live for progressively longer periods on their own and to manage their own life. This is a major psychological move from dependence to independence and establishes a different form of relationship. This new relationship is a dialogue of mutual significance, maintained by signs of care and affection which include now the whole range of physical, verbal, emotional and social affirmation.

Gradually the child separates and learns to register its significance in terms of being cared for by small amounts of physical intimacy and a much greater appreciation mediated through words, feelings and actions.

As we grow towards adulthood, we balance physical closeness and separation between ourselves and those who matter to us and conduct relationships either verbally or through the written word in which we proclaim the mutual importance in terms which signify that we recognise, want and appreciate each other. An essential part of the integrity of personal relationships is the ability to convey and register the appropriate significance of a relationship continuously.

We convey this significance by showing to another person who is important to us the evidence that they remain important in the course of fluctuating circumstances. Integrity requires that we remind the other person of their meaning to us even though we may not see them frequently. There is an obvious lack of credibility when we maintain that we care for another person who does not feature in our life at any other moment except when they are present or when we need something from them or when we have used them and then ignored them.

Integrity and love are closely connected and, in an age where personal relationships are of great importance, we notice soon enough when those who claim to care for or love us ignore us as soon as we are out of sight, or only remember us when we provide a service for them. Integrity is linked with the ability to retain the presence of a significant other in their physical absence.

This is a process which grows from infancy onwards. We can stay for progressively longer periods away from those who matter to us because we form a visual and emotional image of them inside us which acts as a retaining link with them.

In this way we can preserve the ties of friendship and of love in the physical absence of the person. There is a sense of oneness within us as the self and the other are fused in an inner experience that activates meaning, intimacy, affection and the desire for the fullest possible reunion.

St John's Gospel exhibits clearly the presence of the Father in the Son and the dynamic motivating result of this interaction of two persons in one.

> I am the good shepherd,
> I know my own
> and my own know me;
> just as the Father knows me
> and I know the Father.
> And I lay down my life for my sheep. (John 10:14–15)

The ability to carry others inside us is intimately related with our ability to register the signals they give which denote that we matter to them. This acceptance of others is so important that it needs some detailed attention.

Registration of Others

The means of registering others depends on our ability to experience fully another person as they communicate to us physically, emotionally, intellectually, socially and spiritually.

As young children our principal experiences are physical and emotional. We are touched and held and the quality of the physical experience conveys a sense of affectionate and trusting transmission of care. But there are some children, and later on adults, who cannot bear to be touched, who find physical closeness intimidating and who cannot trust those close to them. Thus a lot of messages are simply not recorded.

Verbal messages play a vital role. Our ability to listen to these is the key to registering the importance of the message conveyed. A great deal of our integrity relies on how well we can listen to others, for an accurate and sensitive interpretation of what they are saying is due to them in justice and in love.

Listening of course is much more than hearing words. We need to listen to the meaning behind words and to respond both to the objective message and the affective content. There are men and women who find it very difficult to listen or to record affection. As far as listening is concerned, they wait for the other's sound to cease so that they can have their turn to speak. They reply with no' relevance to what was said to them. They feel criticised and attacked when no such intention exists and they are impervious to appreciation when it is expressed. In the presence of these defects the relationship is barren and there is no possibility of integrity because the other person is simply ignored. This can be deliberate or the individual may have defective abilities in registering the messages from another human being. But in the absence of such an accurate exchange there is also a loss of mutual trust.

Trust and Trustworthiness

Trust and integrity are closely connected. We experience the meaning of trust by noting the way people who claim to care for us behave. Most of us in fact experienced a loving mother who picked us up, fed us, cleaned us, spoke to us and remained reliable and predictable in her nurturing. In this way we come to expect certain characteristics in those we trust. We expect them to be consistent, to tell us the truth, to treat us fairly, to listen to us and respond to our legitimate requests. At a more basic level we need to feel secure, relaxed in their presence and feel that we can trust our body and inner world to their care without fearing betrayal or being let down.

Part of the task of those who care for us is to communicate trust to us and, in doing so, help us to feel trustworthy persons ourselves. It is really vital that the self we possess should feel trustworthy and there is nothing that attacks our integrity more than the realisation that we cannot rely on ourselves to be the sort of person we claim to be.

Fear

There are two factors that commonly corrode our own trustworthiness. The first one is fear. We start life as helpless children who are at the mercy of many who are bigger, stronger, capable of hurting and punishing us, and we live also in a world that has deadly traps for us. We learn from childhood the unpleasantness of pain, be it physical or emotional, particularly if it involves the withdrawal of love of those who matter to us. Throughout our whole life there is a battle to maintain the truth, carry out our promises, disclose the unpleasant part of ourselves, own up when we are in the wrong, and face the consequences whatever these may be. In all these situations, the fear of pain, displeasure and social disgrace may be so overwhelming that we compromise our position. It is worth remembering here the conflict Christ had over his death and the struggle he had to keep his dedicated promise to the Father. 'Abba', he said, 'Everything is possible for you. Take this cup away from me. But let it be as you, not I, would have it' (Mark 14:36).

The sense of self-accepting wholeness which I referred to before preserves us from our fears. If we are totally dependent on others for survival, if we live by kind permission of others, then we risk alienating them. We cannot face the truth with them because we fear that their disapproval will mean the end of us. But if we possess ourselves with a sufficient amount of self-accepting wholeness, then we can accept legitimate criticism and even temporary abandonment because our own resources are sufficient to maintain life in us until the relationship returns to normality.

Anger
The second factor is anger. Some dynamic psychologists claim to have identified aggressive and destructive behaviour in an infant of a few months old. Without discussing this particular theory, there is little doubt that children can experience aggressive feelings very early on in their development. Aggression becomes most evident around the second and third years of life when the child is asserting its first phase of independence and has to challenge mother who wants things done her way. This is the first moment when aggression threatens to hurt, damage or even destroy a person we love. At all stages of our life we are threatened with the anxiety of being overwhelmed by our anger and destroying someone, but particularly those we love.

Yet there is a place and a necessity to express anger at the appropriate moments of our life. When people hurt us we may have to show our anger as a means of bringing to their attention that their behaviour is unacceptable. Clearly there is a very legitimate anger and at times we would be failing our duty if we did not register our protest. Our Lord did not hesitate to show his anger.

> So they reached Jerusalem and he went into the Temple and began driving out those who were selling and buying there; he upset the tables of the money changers and the chairs of those who were selling pigeons. Nor would he allow anyone to carry anything through the Temple. And he taught them and said: Does not scripture say: My house will be called a house of prayer for all the people? But you have turned it into a robber's den. (Mark 11:15–17)

Faced with anger, we run the risk of avoiding expressing it and allowing the wrong to continue. We also run the risk of our anger overwhelming us and actually damaging the other person. Our integrity is connected with both occurrences. If we are afraid to show our anger and frustration, then they can build up in us and lead to worse consequences. If we are overwhelmed by our anger, we damage and we need to repair the damage. Ultimately our integrity lies in being sure that our love is greater than our anger and, whatever the demonstration of the latter, we will not allow a relationship of love to be destroyed.

We have to learn how to handle conflict, guilt and forgiveness without being overwhelmed by the first two and neglecting the latter. We need to forgive not only those who trespass against us; sometimes it is even more important to forgive ourselves. Occasionally others forgive us but we cannot forgive ourselves and remain with the burden of unrelieved guilt. Such persistent feelings of badness lay the foundations of feeling unlovable and prevent us from accepting the love offered to us by others.

Change and Continuity
Forgiving and being forgiven, trusting and being trusted, loving and being loved are all continuous processes which occur throughout our lives. This poses a fundamental ques-

tion, namely how can we go on changing as we do throughout our lives and retain a sense of integrity with those we relate to? This is at the centre of the problem of continuity of relationship with our spouses, commitment to vocation, maintaining interest in our work, remaining loyal to causes, retaining friendships; above all staying faithful to God. Divorce, withdrawal from religious life, boredom with work, abandonment of causes, breakdown of friendships and loss of faith are constant human tragedies which evoke a cry of betrayal and loss of integrity. Some of these changes are due to hasty or faulty original choices which are really incompatible with our personality and a misjudgment is made. But others are authentic choices which reflect accurately our personality at one stage in our life but not at another.

Whilst we retain the same body and intellect, both change; the one ages and the other grows into wisdom, but it is our emotions, feelings and social expectations that change radically. We change from being dependent to being independent. We move from hesitancy to certainty, from passivity to initiative, from impulsiveness to mature judgment, from fear to confidence, from confusion to clarity and so on. Whilst remaining basically the same person in appearance, our inner world of needs, abilities, self-esteem, availability and receptivity all change. Here is one of the greatest challenges to integrity, for we all change and have to do so with the minimum hurt, rejection and betrayal of persons and the maximum alteration of identification with ideas, concepts and things. We change but must not alter in our commitments of love. We have to learn to love in new ways but it is essential that we do not make commitments of love until we are sufficiently free and possess enough of ourselves that we can guarantee a minimum continuity of loving. God's covenant with his people in the Old Testament and Christ's faithfulness to his Father both involve change in the midst of uninterrupted continuity of commitment. Here we are in the very midst of the mystery of love and integrity.

The image of God shines with the integrity of resolute steadfastness whilst man shifts, vacillates, and betrays. The parable of the good shepherd, already quoted, is a good illustration of steadfastness and continuity of life-giving processes.

> I tell you most solemnly,
> I am the gate of the sheepfold.
> All others who have come
> are thieves and brigands;
> but the sheep took no notice of them.
> I am the gate.
> Anyone who enters through me will be safe:
> he will go freely in and out
> and be sure of finding pasture.
> The thief comes
> only to steal and kill and destroy.
> I have come
> so that they may have life
> and have it to the full.
> I am the good shepherd:
> the good shepherd is one who lays down his life for his
> sheep.
> The hired man, since he is not the shepherd
> and the sheep do not belong to him,
> abandons the sheep and runs away
> as soon as he sees a wolf coming,
> and then the wolf attacks and scatters the sheep;
> this is because he is only a hired man
> and has no concern for the sheep. (John 10:7–13)

Integrity in Personal Counselling

The mark of service is personal integrity, one of whose characteristics is faithfulness. But we can remain faithful to another person, committed to their well-being and yet fail to do justice to their needs. So much current service is personal counselling and so it is worth while examining the characteristics of integrity in this area of service.

The traditional characteristics of counselling consist of listening with care, being non-judgmental and avoiding offering advice but instead helping the person to clarify his/her problem and reach an appropriate solution from within their own resources which have now been liberated.

We find some of these features reflected in the scriptures. The counsellor is the person who hears more than words and is open to the whole person, is ready to receive the conscious and the unconscious, the overt and the latent, the grasped and the hidden, the perceived and the omitted. The essential task of listening is to help another person grasp his inner world, get hold of that which is missing and lead on to a further step in wholeness. All of us have the task of revealing to others their fullness and that means that listening is seeing in depth. When the apostles asked our Lord why he spoke in parables, his reply is a subtle one. In a sense he is asking his audience to reflect on the message he is delivering. He wants his words to penetrate deeply into their being so that the transformation he is asking is a synthesis of a deeper layer of truth. God is always asking us to look more deeply at the truth, to avoid reaching superficial conclusions. The people of God were constantly inclined to respond in a limited and superficial way to the truth with which God wished to engage them. They wanted to be told what to do rather than reach the depths of their being and respond from the core of themselves.

So when Christ replies to the apostles as to why he teaches in parables he quotes a marvellous passage from Isaiah:

The reason I talk to them in parables is that they look without seeing and listen without hearing or understanding. So in their case this prophecy of Isaiah is being fulfilled:

You will listen and listen again, but not understand,
see and see again, but not perceive.
For the heart of this nation has grown coarse,
their ears are dull of hearing, and they have shut their eyes,
for fear they should see with their eyes,
hear with their ears,
understand with their heart,
and be converted
and be healed by me. (Matthew 13:13–15; cf. Isaiah 6:9)

The task of the counsellor, indeed the task of each one of us who acts as a healer to each other, is to listen carefully to the person we receive and, through this, help the person to engage

43

much more of himself. Clearly what we see in others reflects our own experiences and the more we possess ourselves, the more we grasp our own humanity the greater is our ability to perceive in others what they cannot see in themselves.

Christ who was the perfect man was able constantly to see and hear the depths of others, recognise what was in them and move in the direction of raising their level of awareness to a more complete state, to a change of heart which allowed a greater reflection of the image of God in their life. St John summarises this beautifully when he said about Jesus: 'He never needed evidence about any man: he could tell what a man had in him' (John 2:25). Our task as counsellors and also in our relationship with others is to get to know what is in them and to help them overcome their limitations, not by criticising, but by evoking a deeper and wider grasp of themselves.

One of the features of counselling is that, beyond listening, we have to be non-judgmental and allow the other person to reach their decisions freely. Neither judgment nor compulsion is part of the integrity of counselling or loving relationships. Right through the gospels we see our Lord preaching the truth and letting it act as a judgment to human behaviour. Towards those that had failed he had a non-judgmental approach.

This is touchingly shown in John when our Lord is faced with the woman who had been caught committing adultery. He finishes his exchange by saying: 'Has no one condemned you?' 'No one sir,' she replied. 'Neither do I condemn you,' said Jesus, 'go away and don't sin any more' (John 8:10-11). He is really saying to the woman that he accepts her unconditionally as a person and invites her to be more fully human.

This invitation is an appeal to her freedom to choose. There is nothing more fundamental in human relationships than the freedom to love. We cannot love through fear or compulsion. We can go through the outer appearance of loving but ultimately we must want to love and this desire springs from the core of our being. When we relate to others in any form of relationship from counselling to personal love, we can only wait for their free response.

We do not possess other people. We must not use physical or psychological pressure, however subtle it is. Ultimately what we want is their free choice of us or what we are offering. We have a good example of this in the gospels in the story of the rich young man. 'Good master, what must I do to inherit eternal life?' Here was a central question and Christ looked at him with love and took the risk of answering fully. After reminding him to keep the commandments he adds: 'Go and sell everything you own and give the money to the poor and you will have treasure in heaven: then come, follow me. But his face fell at these words and he went away sad, for he was a man of great wealth' (Mark 10:17, 21-2). Our Lord took the risk of revealing the whole truth and being rebuffed. He was rebuffed but he respected the freedom of the young man.

Here is yet another lesson in our counselling and loving relationships with one another. The help we have to give depends on the stage of development of the other person. We can give too much of the truth which frightens people and they turn away. The same applies to personal relationships and it is a key to the secret of maintaining relationships. Sometimes we have to be very patient with those we love until they are ready to take the next move of wholeness in their life. So much of unfaithfulness or lack of effective counselling is due to the breakdown of the relationship because we flood the other with our expectations or we promise more than we can fulfil. Keeping the correct pace and remaining in relationship whilst the other has time to catch up and become whole is a way of maintaining relationship. God's patience with his people in the Old Testament and Christ's patience with his apostles are models of being with others who are unable to respond fully. We must neither compromise the freedom of others nor yield to the despair of expecting no change, for our constant love is capable of transforming others even if their pace is not ours.

In these two chapters I have tried to describe authority in terms of personal integrity. In an age in which derived integrity by blind obedience to authority is being increasingly replaced by an autonomous, self-directing ideal, we have the possibility of examining human integrity in terms of the authority we each carry within ourselves by reflecting the image of God's perfection in our being.

Ultimately it is the authority we express through integrity that persuades and reflects the divine in us for others. It is this integrity which unites the authority of any office or position we hold with the reality of living out its meaning in full. It is this integrity that unites the inner and outer person, the private and public figure, and gives us the consistency and continuity of the oneness of our identity. The struggle to maintain this unity and wholeness pervades the whole of our life and our love is constantly subjected to the strains of being false to the promise we offer to others. Certainly our authority is intimately linked with our integrity and the challenge of our age is the transformation of the image of God in man from the derived to the autonomous.

5

The Capacity to Love I:
Love of Self

According to St John, God is love. The significance of this is twofold. For Christians who believe and accept this as a truth revealed by God there is no alternative but to live a life of love. This is the only way to do justice to the reality that we have been invited to be as perfect as our heavenly Father. For the Christian, loving is the principal expression of his faith.

As far as the non-Christian is concerned, there is no revealed connection between love and God. In the process of loving, however, all human beings experience a feeling of the good, a moment of transcendence, of reaching beyond themselves to an unknown world where the material and the immediate are momentarily surpassed. Every moment of authentic love is an expression of something that surpasses human understanding. Whatever form our loving takes, it touches depths of ourselves which humanity has always recognised as reaching beyond this world and connecting us with a mystery of the beyond. Love is the connection that many make between this world and whatever lies in the beyond. It is the common denominator of most religions and the infrastructure of all humanity when it encounters the world of compassion, mercy, generosity, forgiveness, encouragement, caring, healing; in brief, the availability of self to others.

The language of love is full of ideals, perfect ministration and heroism. Indeed there is no end to the ways that love has been described. In our own Western society love is expressed and understood in personal terms. In other societies where the personal does not or is not permitted to loom in a marked way, it is the collective, be it the extended family,

47

the elders, the government or officials, that ministers to the needs of people. For over three centuries Western society has encouraged the personal and interpersonal approach to love as against the collective. Personal love is very much in line with the love of the Trinity, the three distinct persons loving each other and each loving every one of us individually. So it is love experienced in one-to-one relationships which allows us to understand its meaning most fully. This does not mean that personal love exhausts all the possibilities of its meaning. It does not, nor could it, because ultimately God is love and its full meaning will be revealed only in eternity. But we do experience authentic love here and now in our personal relationships and in doing so we encounter God on earth.

This is the moment to say something further about the concept of love and love of self. All of us have been brought up constantly being reminded that love of self is a dangerous condition. Narcissus watching himself in the pool became totally obsessed with himself, hence the expression narcissistic love. We consider that selfishness is an ego-orientated love which puts self before others. The egoist lives entirely for the glory of his ideas and interests. How, we ask, can love of self be anything other than something which is totally wrong? Nevertheless we are invited to love our neighour as ourselves. It seems that loving God and our neighbour is intimately connected with loving ourselves. So there must be a way of loving the self which is neither indulgent nor corrupting. In fact we know that unless we love ourselves we cannot love others.

We need a psychological framework of reference to find the correct explanation. Our capacity to love is intimately related to our personal development and the process of separation from our parents, during which we are differentiated from them by the gradual acquisition of ourselves. We learn to feel that the body is our body, the mind is our mind, the feelings are our feelings, the skills our skills, the competence our competence, the badness our badness. Thus an essential part of our development is the possession of ourselves as distinguished and distinct from our parents, siblings and others. It is only when we possess ourselves that we can give ourselves to others. We can offer but we cannot give any part of ourselves that we do not possess. Incidentally, the process of gaining possession of ourselves goes on throughout our lives but the major acquisition occurs in the first twenty years of our life.

Possession of ourselves is not enough. If what we possess feels wrong, bad, wicked, then we not only try to hide it from others but we also try to hide it from ourselves. What we possess must on balance feel good if we are to make it available to others. Clearly not everything we possess feels good. We have bad things inside us in the form of weaknesses, temptations and propensities for evil. It is part of the process of maturation that we gradually acquire a sense of ourselves and that on balance it feels more good than bad. This is what is meant by love of self. Through love of self we own our being, it feels more good than bad and in this way we can do two things which are essential for loving. First we can make parts or the whole of ourselves available to others. Secondly, we can let others reach parts or the whole of ourselves. The less we own ourselves the smaller is our availability to others. The smaller our possession of ourselves the fewer are the access points into our lives. Others try to touch our body and we recoil in fear. They try to reach our minds and we shut them out through incomprehension and rigidity. They try to evoke our feelings and receive instead our frigidity and aridity. They try to mobilise our social action and we withdraw in fear and isolation.

It is in Jesus Christ that we meet the person who loved himself comprehensively and was totally available to others. He possessed himself fully and could freely give himself up to death for others. He was totally accessible and there was no one, rich or poor, man or woman, child or adult, who could not reach him.

At the very heart of personal love is a bond or attachment between two people. The capacity to respond to another being, be it human or animal, depends on our capacity to relate. We acquire this capacity to relate in the first three months of our life, in the basic attachment formed between mother and child, mediated, according to Bowlby, through the physical dimensions of touch, vision, sound and smell.

Love Unfolding

This is the first encounter of love for all of us. It is within this framework of attachment that the whole mystery of love will gradually be unfolded. The attachment slowly extends to the father, brothers, sisters, 'relatives and other significant people. We learn to fall in love first with our mother and all subsequent episodes of falling in love occur in this way, by touch, vision, sound and smell. We fall in love with a human being through all these ways, but we can also fall in love by using one dimension only, such as vision when we are overwhelmed by the beauty of a scene, by sound when we are captured by music, and in more banal form when food and drink send messages of fragrance.

By forming this attachment, we all start life in a relationship of love. This love is given to us by our parents. It is unconditional. We do not deserve it. We have not earned it. We have not merited it. We can do little about it. This is the way that God loves humanity and it is in a similar manner that our first experience of love begins. This experience is important in several ways.

First of all love enters our life before speech does. So much love is communicated by a look, a touch or even a smell. Indeed our deepest yearning is to be loved without having to clarify our needs. In the depths of men and women there is a desire for instant understanding, as we were understood by our mother and our needs met. Depths of love are conveyed in this way without verbal communication, and much frustration is experienced when we have to spell out what we need. When this happens we feel that the sparkle has gone out of loving, for the blind understanding of our lover is missing. But in love of God all this can take place. We can feel, be heard and understood without uttering a word. Our innermost needs are responded to because God, the source of all love, knows what we need. Freud said that God is the projected father, the universal neurosis. If anything, he is the loving mother and the response to our deepest experience of love. Not that this love with God is easy to discern. We miss touch and vision. We cannot see God, nor can we touch him. So communication can be difficult, hence the extensive attempts to learn how to pray, which is the language of love with God.

The first attachment of love we make is with our mother. We have spent nine months in her womb and our initial two to three years are lived in marked intimacy. During this period there is a fusion between ourselves and our mother in a framework of total dependence. But we cannot remain in this fused state of oneness for ever. It is wonderful, it feels safe, and we run to her instantly whenever there is the slightest threat to our existence. This yearning to fuse with safety, warmth and understanding remains with us all our life. Whenever we are under threat we seek safety, warmth, understanding, and indeed all humanity yearns for an ultimate fusion with the one, however that one is conceived. The One of Christianity is three separate persons and separation is certainly part of human growth.

As mentioned before, by the third year the child acquires a whole range of autonomy. It can speak, walk, eat unassisted, and so on. By this age it can learn to spend a few hours away from mother in a nursery school. This is a vital step for love. By the third year the child develops the ability to internalise mother. Her presence lives within the child and can be carried within, in her physical absence. So the first tentative steps are taken to love and be loved in the physical absence of the beloved. We can see immediately how important this is for our love of God and our experience of his love. It is happening in the physical absence of God, whom we cannot see or touch, and yet we can hold the divine within us. The sacramental presence of the divine bridges the gap, but our capacity to feel loved in the absence of the physical presence of the lover is a quality we begin to develop by our third year. However we have a long way to go to perfect it.

The separation continues when we go to school and spend an even greater part of the day away from mother. It takes a further fundamental step forward at about eight to ten years of age. The child recognises distinctly the difference between itself and parents. It begins to assert independence in thought and judgment and does not take the given of authority as a granted truth. Children begin to judge and evaluate from now on, and separate further intellectually.

This process continues and reaches its peak in the second half of the second decade when an adult emerges, having completed enough of the process of detachment physically, intellectually and emotionally to begin to lead a separate life. But although separation appears complete at this point, it goes on throughout life as each one of us gradually loses bits of our personality which are parental and authoritarian intrusions, and replaces them by our own evaluations, judgments, sense of right and wrong, priorities, values, attitudes and opinions.

Personhood

The separation which is completed in our teens allows us to become a person with our own boundaries and we are ready to love others. We possess ourself and are ready to give it to others. We fall in love and gradually come to love others. In this love we are completely separate and yet we draw near to the ultimate fusion with the one we love. This can be a spouse, friend, God. Loving is a series of experiences of separateness and oneness, and the dangers of loving lie within these extremes. At one end we preserve our separateness at any price and do not allow others to get close. We are afraid of being taken over or swallowed up by others. At the other end we long to lose our separateness and become one with a significant other. The dangers of these two extremes are that on the one hand we avoid closeness, and on the other we want to recapture oneness at the risk of losing our autonomy. The model of loving is the Trinity in which persons remain in relationship without losing their separate identity, and yet are one in absolute love.

As we separate from mother we gradually lose the physical intimacy of touch. Looks and sounds remain to familiarise us with love, but in fact other experiences extend the feeling of being loved beyond touch, looks, sounds and smell. Gradually we begin to learn that we matter to our parents. We do not matter because we are their possession or property. We do not matter because we are a source of productivity. We do not matter because we are successes. We matter because we are their child. How do we recognise this fact?

We recognise this because we are acknowledged daily. In

their presence we feel that we have a special significance. The relationship present provides a mutual recognition which makes us feel that we have a particular place in their life. Beyond acknowledgment we feel wanted. Our presence is not a matter of indifference to our parents. Rather we feel that our presence is desired and welcomed.

Finally, beyond acknowledgment and feeling wanted we feel appreciated. This appreciation does not depend on any particular ability on our part to provide entertainment. We are not appreciated because we stimulate interest. We may do that but this is incidental. We are appreciated because we are a significant person in the life of our parents.

All this happens in normal homes in the course of normal development. There are many men and women who grow up without feeling they matter. They do not feel acknowledged. Instead they have grown up with a feeling of insignificance. They do not feel wanted, indeed they feel unwanted or rejected, and far from feeling appreciated they feel worthless. These are the wounded men and women who emerge into adolescence neither possessing nor loving themselves. They form the populations of the lonely, the isolated and the vulnerable in marriage and religious life, the socially undesirables, all of whom want love but can neither feel, register nor retain it.

Feeling Bad

These men and women who have grown up without feeling lovable have severe problems in forming relationships of love. The reasons why they grew up feeling unloved are legion. Their parents may not have loved them; a brother or a sister may have been preferred. Their childhood may have been interrupted by long separation from the parents who may have been ill, absent or inept. They may have grown up in a house full of quarrels and friction where no love existed. One or both parents may have died and the step-parent was unloving. They may have had to be taken away and put into a home. On the other hand, none of this may have prevailed. Love may have been present and the child could not register it. Whatever the reason, the danger is that the child will interpret the lack of love as due to its own fault. It will blame itself, and feels bad for its state. It will feel it is its own fault that it is unlovable.

The consequences of this pattern of growth are monumental. These are men and women who are extremely deprived of love. They are very hungry for love but they interpret their need as a selfish desire. They feel bad for needing and feel that they do not deserve any love. They assert and reassert that what they want is wrong and forbidden and the way they feel is their fault. They seek humility, self-abnegation, denial and sacrifice in order to become more acceptable but they can never succeed. They cannot overcome their feelings of badness which return repeatedly and hit them like a boomerang. As a result they choose a spouse who does not love them, treats them badly and humiliates them. They may enter religious life and seek asceticism, blind obedience, conformity, anything in fact which pleases, in order to feel accepted. Some of these people spend their whole life seeking love and acceptance without ever being able to achieve it. Without realising it, they seek adversity, misfortune and all forms of annihilation because deep inside them they do not feel they deserve anything better. They place the cross on their back, not as an instrument of love and liberation but as an engagement to the slavery of rejection. The ultimate tragedy is suicide, which is their way of concluding what they consider to be the nuisance of themselves. This is one ultimate conclusion and one can only hope that God in his infinite love will bestow upon them in the next world what they missed in this.

The outcome is not inevitable. The next solution has its own painful price. These are the people who gradually come to realise that their courtship with humiliation, suffering and a sense of badness is not warranted. It dawns upon them slowly, or sometimes suddenly, that their self-rejection is not justified. They realise that they have been cheated of what is their natural right. They are overwhelmed by an immense sense of anger towards parents, their spouse, their superior, the Church, God, in fact everybody who they believe has colluded with the huge deceit in their life. They insist that those who proclaim to have loved them should have helped them to realise that it was not their fault they felt bad, and should have retrieved the situation for them. Marriages break down, religious depart from their vocation, the Church is hated and God abandoned in a blind rage of fury at feeling let down by all the significant people in their life.

The lessons for Christianity are immense. A faith which has the cross and sacrifice as precious symbols must realise that these are effective only when there is a basic self-acceptance and love of self. The hatred of self and the body is a Gnostic evil and has no fundamental alliance with Christianity. When we are selecting people for religious life we need not only to consider their age and maturity but also their basic self-acceptance and we must be extremely cautious of marked humility, conformity, denial, obedience and self-criticism. These are men and women who have neither sufficient autonomy nor self-acceptance and neither are suitable for religious life.

But what about the bad side of ourselves? Are we not tempted towards self-indulgence, selfishness, laziness, anger, irritability, greed, power, injustice and many other short-comings? Of course we are. Our nature is a fallen one and is prone to weakness, disorder and ultimately chaos. But we have been created in the image of God and therefore our fundamental orientation is towards the good, something that baptism, entering into the life of Christ, reinforces. Our definition of sin is missing the mark or point. The mark or point is love. Fundamentally our badness is not the extent of the wickedness of a debased creature but the failure of a redeemed, adopted son of God to love. Our faith is not a competition of wickedness but a struggle for perfection. The measure of our badness is the absence of love and our first responsibility is the love of self as described in this chapter. If we feel fundamentally good and on balance more good than bad, which is what our life of grace should give us, then we are equipped to deal with our badness. Our badness is the shortcoming of our loving of self and neighbour. We shall deal with love of neighbour in chapter six, but we must also be in a position to forgive ourselves as well. We need to forgive ourselves repeatedly, we need to seek God's forgiveness repeatedly in the knowledge that he forgives those he loves, which is everyone. If he forgives us, we can forgive ourselves and lose the sense of guilt which prevents us from loving. Guilt is a reminder that we have to love more not less. This means treating ourselves with sufficient care to prepare us for as much loving as possible. In being kind to ourselves we are not being soft nor indulgent, we are reducing the sense of alienation within ourselves so that our wholeness and integrity can be preserved and grow for the task of loving.

Hope and Despair

The balance between love of self and self-rejection is also ultimately the balance between hope and despair. We can go on loving ourselves and others until the end of time. No matter what disappointment, frustration or catastrophe comes to our life we can retain the love of God for ourselves and the hope that loving has no end, as indeed St Paul suggests, for when faith and hope are ultimately completed only love will be left. But in this world faith, hope and love are a triad that operate in unison. Faith teaches us to love and hope preserves our inspiration and reminds us that there is no end to loving. Despair on the other hand is an experience which is for ever restricting our capacity to find meaning in ourselves or others. In despair we embrace meaninglessness. There is simply no point in having life and enhancing the life of others. Life has no hope and no meaning and from this springs euthanasia, suicide, abortion, the destruction of life and the constant threat of global annihilation.

Our faith, which is one of love, is the buoy that keeps us afloat in the darkness of desolation and despair. But this faith is rooted in self-acceptance, for without personal meaning the world makes no sense. Our meaning finds its ultimate explanation in a God who is love and the springs of our capacity to be God-like are our potential for loving.

All we know about loving starts from the love we have experienced in our own life, from the love which we feel penetrates our being. It is that love which we understand and can offer to others. The way we offer it to others will be the subject of the next chapter.

6

The Capacity to Love II: Love of Neighbour

Possession of Self
In chapter five the theme of loving oneself was outlined. It was emphasised that this love consisted essentially of the sense of possessing oneself positively so as to be at the service of others. The supreme model of this love is Jesus Christ. This affirmative awareness of self is not an inwardly directed love. The possession of ourselves is primarily justified by facilitating our ability to make our person readily available to others. This distinction is fundamental and it is not readily understood by many Christians who emphasise the diminution of self as the ideal. Diminution is associated with humility but true humility is an authentic appreciation of ourselves in a way that neither exaggerates nor underestimates what we are. Loving is not about contracting but rather about expanding the sense of ourselves and of others. Our age in particular is seeking an expansion of its horizons of the meaning of being. Christianity can answer the call by indicating that the essence of love is the fullness of being, which reflects the image of God, who is love.

Liking
When we discuss love and loving there is a visible tension in any group of people. Not only does everybody know how difficult loving is, but there is also confusion between liking and loving. How can we love the neighbour we do not like? Or the neighbour with whom we have no relationship? We are asked to love everyone but how can we love men and women we have never seen, our overseas neighbour for example? This is a recurrent challenge to the Christian. How

57

can we love the unknown? Someone we neither know nor like?

The distinction between liking and loving is important. We like somebody in whom we recognise features we appreciate. We may be attracted by somebody's body, mind, social characteristics or feelings. We like what we see, hear, touch and feel. This liking is a form of compatibility. We feel comfortable in the presence of someone we like and we share a kindred spirit of either similarity or complementarity. That which attracts us may be someone who is similar to us or who completes us in some way.

Liking another person depends on receiving signals which make sense to some part of ourselves. The experience may be transient or continuous. We may like a little or a lot but our world does not collapse if we lose the person we like. Such loss can cause distress but we have no profound expectations from those we like. We are surrounded by people and things we like and all of them give us pleasure. But the degree of engagement of our being and our obligations are quite different for those we love.

Love
The first thing to appreciate about loving is that we may or may not like the person we love. Indeed we may not even know the actual person. We could not love our overseas neighbour, or the unseen and unknown mystery of God if love depended on liking each and everyone we love. In this way love becomes a means of universal attachment. International peace and justice are part of this universal love, for everyone needs peace, freedom and justice as the background within which personal love can flourish.

But for most of us the neighbour we have the challenge of loving is someone close to us, our parents, spouse, relatives, friends or members of our community. It is someone we recognise, want and appreciate as a significant other whose loss leaves a profound vacuum in our life. When we move from liking to loving, the loved one becomes a significant person whose involvement with our life now matters a great deal. This significant connection is established by forming a commitment to love. We do not form a commitment to like.

We either like or we do not, we cannot really dictate the sensation. But loving is another matter. If we do love someone or something, we make a commitment to that person or cause. What are the characteristics of commitment?

Commitment

In everyday language we refer to loyalty to a cause or person. By loyalty we mean that we neither betray nor abandon our commitment. In fact one of the essential features of commitment is continuity. We love others when they begin to experience from us the sense of continuous availability. All of us would like to feel that we can turn to those we love at any time and find them ready to respond. We are not always ready to like but loving is a summons we cannot ignore. So continuity is the first criterion of commitment.

We can of course offer continuity which does not answer the needs of the loved one. We can be available all the time without offering a reliable response. We intend to please, to satisfy, to meet the loved one's needs but we achieve none of these things because there is a gap between what we intend and what we can achieve. We promise, we mean what we promise, but we do not deliver the goods. This is where the possession of ourselves is markedly defective and so we raise expectations and then let down the people we love. All of us know people with excellent intentions who promise so much and fulfil so little. They live a life in which excuses become second nature. Gradually the one we love knows to expect a very small portion of what we promise. This is unlike God, who is always available and continuously reliable. He can be trusted and trust is an essential part of reliability.

To continuity and reliability, we need to add predictability. We cannot love others if we are totally unpredictable. This does not mean that pleasant surprises are not welcome. But we need to be able to gauge with reasonable accuracy the response of those who claim to love us. Loving needs a secure background and that is where predictability comes into its own. If we are truly loving we offer to our loved ones behaviour which makes sense to them. We expect a smile to be followed by some kind action, not by a storm of abuse. We expect those who love us not to let us down when we rely on their accustomed behaviour. Both personal and public life depends on taking certain things for granted and predictability is an essential infrastructure of order. If we love, we do not suddenly stop loving. If we care, we do not suddenly stop caring. Our life of love relies on predictability. When predictability ceases, then love is no longer possible. We expect our spouse to be faithful. We expect our friends to be loyal. We expect our parents to be supportive. Children need predictable parents and teachers. Patients need predictable doctors. At the very centre of loving, there is the discharge of the expected and when this cannot be relied upon, loving ceases too.

But what do we need continuity, reliability and predictability for? These three qualities form the framework of loving intimacy between two people. Without these features there is no relationship which can maintain the channels of loving. But given that these channels are open, what are the features of loving that occur within the relationship? I have selected four features which all of us can identify as loving, namely affirmation, sustaining, healing and growth and I want to describe each in turn.

Affirmation

It will be remembered that an essential part of learning to love ourselves is to be helped to possess ourselves in an affirmative manner. As parents we help our children to feel their growing parts are their own and that their possession is good. Likewise teachers help children to acquire intellectual, physical, social, emotional and spiritual qualities and to realise that their use is creative and loving. We help those under our care to find themselves and feel pleased with their unfolding awareness. Spouses do likewise to each other. God the Father affirmed his Son at his baptism and at the transfiguration. God's love for his Son was continuous and our affirmation has to be continuous.

At this point, you may search your memory in vain to know when you were last affirmed. What you remember are the endless points that have been made to you regarding your shortcomings. It would seem that most of us are much more accustomed to be loved via criticism. People feel that they help us best by pointing out what is missing or defective in our make-up. But that is not the basic way of loving. We need to look at the potential of people and gradually enhance it. If we only criticise, we focus on the negative elements and emphasise fear and guilt. We know from St John that perfect love and fear are incompatible and so our loving must not, as far as possible, rely on fear.

By affirming others we give them the feeling that we love what we find in them. Gradually and within a framework that enhances the good, we can agree on the bits that are undesirable and try to eliminate them. The best way to diminish deficiency is by expanding that which is positive and loving in each one we relate to.

Sustaining

One way of affirming others is by sustaining them. We sustain people socially in demanding or adverse situations. But undoubtedly it is emotional sustaining that makes the hardest demands on us. Men and women turn to us for loving in a variety of situations. They may be going through a confused period of their life such as their adolescence or retirement. We are asked to sustain those who have suffered a loss through bereavement or whose spouse has left them, those who have lost status, position and employment. We have to love men and women until they rediscover their way and meaning in life. We have to love those who have experienced a loss until their grief passes and they are prepared to enter the world once again. We have to sustain the alienated and the dispossessed.

Sustaining in these situations means that we become the centre of loving for these men and women. For those who are confused we become their beacon of light. We hold their hand until they find their feet. We give them meaning from our inner world because they cannot find meaning in their own life. We become a source of comfort until the loss can be integrated in the stricken ones. We offer acceptance to those who have lost their dignity through no fault of their own. In order to do these things, we have to possess the strength to guide without intrusion, to comfort by sharing the grief, to accept the dignity of all men and women independently of their social status. Such sustaining means that for long periods we give and may receive very little back. We are often reminded of the grandeur of giving. But as we have shown we cannot give unless we have the inward resources to make ourselves available, even in the absence of immediate recompense.

In particular sustaining the confused, the mourners and the dispossessed is difficult. All of them are likely to become depressed and in the midst of their depression they feel unlovable, unwanted, negative and unreachable. Some of these men and women we try to console may in fact reject our efforts to comfort them. They may not be able to accept what we offer to them. They may be steeped in so much gloom that all hope is resisted. In brief, we may find that our efforts to sustain are spurned and rejected. We have very good reason and justification to stop our effort but that is where continuous sustaining remains important. Within the boundaries of the freedom of the individual, that is to say so long as people accept our sustaining, loving demands that we continue to give it independently of the response. The only restriction is when we conclude that our sustaining actually reinforces the distress, in circumstances where the person consciously uses our support in order not to change.

Healing

The essence of sustaining is to remain in relationship and by doing so love continues to flow between two people. Sustaining however needs to give way to healing when we love those who are wounded. As mentioned in chapter two, the wounded are those who have inherited characteristics of a painful nature, such as excessive anxiety, or a tendency towards depression, or those who have been brought up in a neglecting or rejecting environment. I am often asked whether there is anything we can do for these wounded human beings and the answer is yes.

Healing demands all the characteristics of love mentioned so far. There is a need for continuity in the relationship with reliable and predictable behaviour. Healing takes place in two ways. The lover becomes the person who offers a second opportunity, a second chance to the wounded person who now knows for the first time what it feels like to be acknowledged, wanted and appreciated. Within the framework of this acceptance, the wounded acquire a new experience of themselves. They learn for the first time in adulthood what they missed in childhood. This is the positive acquisition of new characteristics. There is also the gradual extinction of undesirable characteristics. By being reliable and predictable, we can help people to lose some of their anxiety features and to learn that depression is not an inevitable accompaniment of their life.

Thus healing is offering ourselves in loving acceptance of others by taking the place of the original significant figures who let them down. Healing is not easy because the wounded are expecting to be abandoned, rejected, hurt and are likely to interpret the slightest mistake on our part as a recurrence of their original fear. Gradually, however, we can persuade them that we are reliable and predictable lovers and they can find in us what they missed in their parents.

The important point to make is that healing is not an intellectual conversion. We cannot heal people by telling them what to do. Emotional healing is the acquisition of loving experiences and the extinction of negative, rejecting ones. It is only another human being who can do this for us in the here and now. God of course is the supreme healer. He helps us to heal others and is the source of all healing in himself. His healing has no human limitations but in essence it operates through his unbounded availability. He is available in a reliable and predictable manner and he makes a covenant with humanity which is never broken. This covenant is affirmed in Jesus Christ and so all of us who have access to the fellowship of the Trinity can be healed.

Growth

Healing overlaps with growth. Growth continues throughout our life and it is based ultimately on realising our potential. Men and women come to us wounded, in the sense that they have yet to realise their independence, the sense of their worth, the ability to evaluate and trust their judgment, frightened that they will collapse in a heap through their inadequacies. Before we can facilitate growth we have to restore these qualities in their life. Thus we have to help them out of their extreme dependence on us. We encourage them to think and act of their own accord and to trust their judgments. They will make mistakes but, with constant encouragement, they will find themselves. Having reached the stage of development appropriate for their age, then we can encourage further growth. In the physical, social and intellectual spheres we can encourage others to convert the qualities they already possess into something better. More importantly, in the emotional sphere, our capacity to love grows deeper with time and knows no end.

Through our love of others, but particularly those who we know well, we can avoid the comments that hurt, the sly criticism, the dismissive remark, the exclusion, the pleasantries in front of them and the poison in their absence. We can praise instead of criticising, share joy and sorrow; we can empathise. In this way, little by little, we acquire insight into the very core of being of those we love so that we offer to them, as accurately as possible, what they need from us. There is no end to our capacity for loving and promoting and facilitating full growth in all those we love.

Difficulties in Loving

All of us can recognise sustaining, healing and the facilitation of growth of others but we realise that we have shortcomings in loving. What are the difficulties in loving?

Those who are hurt do not accept love easily. They live in a world which has conditioned them to feel rejected and unwanted. Thus there are those who find it difficult to allow us to love them, instead of realising that our efforts are directed at their acceptance, they feel we could not possibly mean that. Everyone in their life has, so far, rejected them and they do not know what acceptance means. They repulse our love. We try to make them feel significant in our life and they feel ignored. We try to understand them and they feel misunderstood. We try to avoid judgment and they feel both judged and misjudged.

This persistence on our part is a key element in loving. Persisting in loving someone who will not accept our loving is extremely difficult. In fact the whole of the Old and New

Testament is about this kind of love which is divine in nature. God of the Old Testament and Christ both tasted humanity's rejection of their love, but they persisted and persist. Human frailty circumscribes persistence. To go on offering our love which is thrown back in our face is a supremely divine quality and it is hard to imitate. Our persistence diminishes, our efforts wane both when our love is rejected and when we see no results. Our persistence is eroded in everyday life even when those we love respond.

Another reason why we find loving fatiguing is that some people need constant reminders of our love. They accept our loving feelings but their registration of them is poor. They cannot internalise the love we offer. They keep asking for reassurance and we get angry that they do not believe us. We feel children need repetition but not adults. One word, signal or action should be sufficient to indicate that we love them. But their retention is poor and they need to be told repeatedly. We feel that our efforts are a waste of time and yet they are not, because these men and women quickly feel empty. We know that God never ceases to try to give us what we need even though we neither recognise it nor retain it.

That leads us into another difficulty in loving. God knows what is good for us but we do not necessarily know what is good for our neighbour unless we listen very carefully to their inner world. We need to be aware of the real needs of those we love; not what we think is good for them; not even necessarily what they think is good for themselves. If we communicate accurately we will come to understand the real needs, hopes and aspirations of the person. Sometimes people are confused and cannot offer a proper insight into their situation. This is where loving ensures that we do not fill them up with our ideas of what is appropriate for them. Rather we need to facilitate their own unique development of themselves. Sometimes we run into difficulties with communication because those we love expect us to know what is good for them without disclosing it. They are emotionally at a stage when our love has to recapture the characteristics of mother who 'knew' what we needed without having to be told.

At other times we get really confusing messages from others. Men and women appear on the surface to be self-sufficient, efficient and effective, in control of their lives and needing nothing. We assume their strength and we have no idea that behind their façade they are really in need of affection. These are the disciplined, organised persons who give no hint of their underlying fragility. Then an event occurs, such as illness or a loss or the assumption of a pressurising task, and their integration is splintered. We cannot really believe that they are the same people. It is a good reminder that those who appear to be strong and need no one are in fact vulnerable underneath and we should not be surprised if suddenly their anxiety and insecurity overwhelms them.

Finally we go through periods in our own life when we feel empty and have nothing to give. We may be depressed, ill, worn out, tired, disenchanted, disappointed and lacking in hope. We feel that nobody wants us and we radiate negativity. We want to run away and hide because we have nothing to offer. This is a time to remind ourselves that what we have to offer is ourselves. When we were babies all that we had to offer was our presence to mother. The same applies in life later on when sometimes all we have to offer is ourselves, until such time as the sense of our value returns.

Offering ourselves, even though we feel a vacuum within, is an authentic form of loving. There are, however, inauthentic forms of loving.

The first one is idealised love, that is to say we look up to somebody and put them on a pedestal. Nothing is too good for them. They inspire us, they become our idol. Love in these circumstances becomes a tribute to greatness, mingled with fear. We look up and see greatness, we look down and see ourselves. We put a specific barrier between the idol and ourselves. We exaggerate their qualities and find nothing wrong with them as people. They are the source of all wisdom, power and perfection and we live through them. One spouse may idealise the other. Children idealise parents, pupils their teacher, athletics their heroes, those under authority the source of authority and so on. Idealisation places people beyond us and we wonder at their greatness from afar. But woe to them if they make a mistake or they fall from their pedestal. Then we turn on them with fury because they have no business to let us down. Idealised love has no room for defect or error. The idol must be perfect or else they are nothing.

Idealisation however has other problems. We gaze with admiration at our idol but we seethe with envy underneath. We want to be like them and we cannot wait our turn to smash the idol and take its place. We gaze with wonder but we are also afraid that we might displease and incur the punishment of the idol. The gods of Greece and Rome were idealised from afar and also feared. Dictators are idealised and also feared. But Jesus Christ offered to become like one of us. He insisted that he was equal in everything except sin. So God does not demand idealisation, though far too many still idealise, in an infantile way, the priestly representatives of the church from priest to pope.

We aim to love people unconditionally but, if it is for their attributes, then we are looking for authenticity and integrity. We are looking for men and women whose inner and outer life match. That happened supremely in Jesus Christ. He invites us to love him, not to put him on a pedestal and be ready to smash him when we have outlived the usefulness of his grandeur.

Another form of false loving is expressed in jealousy. The essential mark of jealousy is the fear that we shall lose someone we love to a third party. We are expecting to be abandoned at any time, to be left for somebody else, to be excluded by the entry of a third person. Therefore we restrict the life of the person we love so that they have no access to others. We are suspicious of their slightest change in behaviour which we interpret as the first sign of our dismissal. So we try to possess them and to restrict their lives in every possible form until they have no outlet except for us. We ask where they go, who they see, what they do and harass them with our intrusions. Gradually they feel our prisoners and are afraid to do anything of their own accord. At its extreme end, jealousy is not relieved even by these measures. We remain sure that we are going to be betrayed and we interpret the behaviour of our lover in this way, however innocent they may be. The ultimate act of jealous folly is the Othello syndrome, the actual destruction of the one we love but cannot trust. In fact the person we cannot trust is ourselves but we have no insight to that and so we project our betrayal to others. The jealousy of the triangular situation is permanently corrected by the mutual trust and faithfulness of the Trinity. The Father loves and trusts the Son. The Son loves and trusts the Father. Both love and trust the Spirit which is the fruit of their love and the Spirit responds back in absolute trust.

Finally there is the love we all offer and in fact rarely realise that it is no love at all. This is the false love, already mentioned, in which we fashion people after our own image. We fill their emptiness with our own ideas of what they should be. This sort of brainwashing goes on in many parts of the world.

People come to us confused and, instead of helping them to find themselves, we indoctrinate them with our ideas. We give them what we think they need. We do not listen to their pleas for clarification. We give them premasticated food which we believe is essential for them. We create them in our own imperfect image. This is no facilitation of development but brainwashing, and we brainwash them according to our interpretation of the truth. This is of course the difference between giving advice and counselling. Advice is the fruit of our own experience, what suits us. But each one of us is unique and what suits us may not be the appropriate course for another person. In counselling, we consider a variety of ideas and see which one best fits the person. But we encourage the decision to be theirs, we do not live their life for them.

This has enormous implications for all of us who have others under our care. It is tempting to offer what has been tried and proved successful in our life. But what we have to do is to discern accurately their style of life and try to offer ideas of what might suit them, always of course encouraging their free decision to evaluate, choose and assess whether something fits their personality. The supreme act of love is to ensure the constant freedom of those we serve. This is how God loves us and this is how we have to love others.

This can of necessity be only a small part of what love is. What I have tried to stress is that loving means making ourselves available to others in a variety of ways which complete the wholeness and authenticity of those we love. In order to love, we must possess ourselves as fully as possible because loving is offering ourselves to others. The more we possess ourselves the better we can reach others. Possession of ourselves is not a once and for all event. We lose and find ourselves constantly. We add and subtract from ourselves continuously. We fluctuate in our self possession and availability. Our loving, hopefully, is constant but often it is not. We need not lose heart, because we can pick up our intention of loving at any moment and start afresh. We have as our supreme example the continuity and constancy of God to imitate. Our loving is patchy, uneven and for some periods it ceases to exist. But at the very centre of our Christian being is the agape of God which has, like God, no beginning and no end. We share in this agape which is our constant fuel. We can go on loving until the end of our life, with God until the end of time and beyond when all reality will be love in relationship.

7

Freedom and Integrity I

This is an age in which the freedom of the individual is considered to be of great importance. At a political level the West is deeply concerned about the freedom of citizens in the Communist countries, in South Africa or Latin America. There is world wide concern for civil rights. This quest for freedom is not confined to the political sphere. It spreads into the world of women and their emancipation, the rights of minority groups, the needs of the handicapped and the oppressed.

There is, however, a sense of oppression which may be identified within ourselves. Our freedom in relation to our aggressive and sexual instincts was the concern of Freud but there are many other psychological realities which are part of our daily experience and which appear to be, at the very least, distorted.

As far as freedom is concerned, our society defines broad parameters of what is considered permissible within which our individual personality functions. This personality derives its freedom from the make-up of the individual, inherited from the parents, and the atmosphere in which each person grows in the home.

The freedom we acquire has the possibility to be as nearly fully human as possible or it can be severely disturbed. By integrity I mean several things: first that our experience of freedom in a particular dimension achieves its objective as fully as possible; for example, that our capacity to trust is truly experienced without limitations or distortions; secondly, that the experience is lived in depth, in other words, it is wholly accessible in our life and is not buried in our unconscious or excluded from our conscious. Thirdly and finally, integrity means that, beyond having access to our experiences, beyond ensuring that they achieve their objective, they are creative and loving in spirit. Integrity is access, balance, wholeness and affirmation.

Let us now look at some of the crucial aspects of our personality with these features in mind.

Attachment
At the very beginning of our life we form an attachment or a bond with our mother, then with our father, brothers and sisters and other relatives.

This attachment is formed through touch, vision and sound. We are held and we hold our mother. We see and we are seen by her. She speaks to us and, in due course, we speak back to her. These are the basic means by which we form all our subsequent attachments. In the process of forming an attachment we are attracted by the body of another person. We like to get close to it and touch it. We like to look and gaze at each other and finally we like to speak and be spoken to. In this way we become connected with another person.

In theory we have the possibility of forming many attachments and, in fact, we do so in practice. There are social restrictions which some societies impose. Colour, caste, religion, status and class ensure that we can be limited in our range of choice. But even within the categories we are free to participate in, there are restrictions in terms of our own make-up.

Some people find it difficult to experience close physical encounter. These are men and women who find physical closeness threatening and so their ability to form intimate relations is restricted. Some find it very difficult to look into the eyes of another person. They get anxious and distressed and try to hide their gaze from others. Finally some people find it very difficult to listen to or to communicate with others. Thus at the physical level integrity requires the ability to get close, see and be seen; talk and be talked to without anxiety rising to the point where it is necessary to disengage. The anxious, frightened, insecure and those lacking self-esteem want to run away from others.

Quality of Attachment

Given that there is ample freedom to form an attachment physically, the matter does not rest there. In the encounter of human attachment, feelings are involved. Physical, visual and auditory sensations are pleasant and give an underlying gratification for which attachment is sought. But the freedom to form a physical attachment does not exhaust the possibility of the encounter of two people. Within the encounter of mother and child, the latter begins to feel recognised, wanted and appreciated. It feels recognised by associating the presence of mother with tender language and the sense of being wanted by the readiness with which its needs are met. It feels appreciated because the encounter is linked with affirmative signals indicating that its presence gives joy to the parent. The mother puts herself at the disposal of the infant, thus making her availability a gift to her child.

The need for physical encounters to be surrounded with a qualitative acceptance continues in all relationships and in adult life. Most people have the ability to establish a physical relationship but this is not enough. They have to surround it with positive feelings and here there may be a substantial gap between the bodily and emotional encounter. Men and women may find it difficult either to make themselves available or to demonstrate affection.

The person who finds it difficult to be available is judged to be lazy and selfish, but laziness and selfishness need further understanding. Such a person may have been brought up in an environment where all the initiative was held by one parent who was the dominant one. Such a mother or father needed to have absolute control and take charge of everything. Their children grew up feeling that initiative was dangerous and forbidden. Some children grow up in a home where demonstration of affection is severely lacking. In their upbringing they did not see their parents hugging, kissing or exchanging sweet pleasantries with each other. On the contrary, such a household only exchanged comments which were critical and led to admonition of each other. Children growing up in such environments come to their own relationships later on unable to show interest, take care of others or show their affection. They are prisoners of their past. When they are accused of being lazy or indifferent, they know in their heart of hearts that this is not the case but they do not have the emotional freedom to demonstrate their care.

At the extreme end of this lack of freedom and integrity is the man who goes to the prostitute and pays for the physical encounter without any emotional involvement, which is beyond his reach. The client-prostitute encounter is the extreme end of all relationships, in which one or both people use each other for sex, security, reassurance, to ward off loneliness but who cannot extend the attachment to recognition, acceptance or appreciation.

Social attachments at work, in groups or clubs, do not require much beyond the physical contact and the assumption of the social roles for the occasion. But all attachments of friendships, marriage and love require the freedom to initiate the attachment and the emotional dimension to maintain it. Here we meet some of the problems of lack of integrity in our age which are all attempts to escape the conjunction between the physical and emotional unity of relationship. Thus the transient and the disposable are some of the heresies of our age. Men and women live together without marriage because they do not want to commit themselves to a permanent union. They want the freedom to enter and leave relationships without any responsibility. In other words, to have the freedom to move from one relationship to another when they cannot negotiate the emotional integrity.

But at the very heart of relationship is continuity and reliability. The child needs both these qualities in order to survive, grow and be nurtured. But it is not only the child who needs this quality of permanency – all relationships need it. It is only within the context of continuity that our abilities to recognise, want and appreciate develop. It takes time to learn all the needs of our friends, lovers and spouses so that they feel recognised. It takes time to understand how they want to be wanted and appreciated. Thus permanency is a feature of integrity in relationship and it is compared and contrasted with transience that extracts from a relationship all it can and abandons the task of giving back.

Thus the freedom to form relationships is intimately related

73

to the physical and emotional consequences which need continuity for integrity.

Trust

One of the essential features of relationship and its integrity is mutual trust between the persons concerned. In social terms disloyalty, betrayal and treason are social characteristics which are repugnant to human integrity. At the personal and interpersonal level, trust is of paramount importance.

The young child experiencing physical and emotional attachment learns the rudiments of trust very early on. It experiences a feeling of safety in the arms of its mother and gradually this physical trust is extended in the recognition that develops at a distance between child and mother. There is built a unity of trust. The child trusts mother that it will not be condemned physically or emotionally and the mother guarantees this exchange. Trust is the beginning of faith and it is an essential characteristic of all loving relationships. In the presence of trust the relationship is validated in its authenticity.

However, mistrust can easily enter the life of the child. It can have the bad luck of being reared by a mother who batters it. Instead of affection, this child learns that aggression is the sign of its acceptance. Or such a child can have the misfortune of being abandoned or rejected by its parents, so it spends its life in an institution or moves from relative to relative. The absence of a safe physical and emotional attachment primes such a person to regard its surrounding world with suspicion. Instead of security it acquires the fear of being abandoned, unwanted or rejected. This fear becomes gradually a part of its life so that it expects those close to it to act in a similar manner. Such a person expects to be let down, rejected, hurt, attacked or even destroyed by others. They are particularly vulnerable to suspicion about the intentions of others. Such vulnerable people find it hard to establish relationships of trust and both their freedom and integrity of relating are restricted.

Self-esteem

As has been described before, we grow and become increasingly aware of ourselves, the experiences we have at the hands of our parents become vital for the image we form of ourselves. Thus if we feel recognised, wanted and appreciated we tend to feel that we have a positive meaning for our parents. We approach them with the certainty that we are lovable. If we feel trust, this makes us experience ourselves as trustworthy and reliable. It is this accumulation of positive feelings which builds our self-esteem. At this early stage in our life our good feelings about ourselves are built on the unconditional acceptance of our parents. We do not have to earn our good feelings. Our self-esteem is not built on the results of our endeavours. It is based on the gift of our parents cherishing us. This desire for unconditional acceptance permeates the very core of our being and surfaces whenever we encounter true love. This desire surfaces in close friendships, courtship and marriage when a couple want to be cherished as a person, for what they are, not for what they do, achieve or the degree they please. In the core of our being all of us want to re-experience unconditional lovability and ultimately it is the presence of this that gives the deep joy of peace in the presence of those who love us. This is the ultimate integrity of interpersonal acceptance and it is amply demonstrated in the Son-Father relationship of the Trinity.

It is an integrity, however, which is not easy to realise. As we go to school, grow older, involve ourselves further in society, we discover the world of effort and reward. Our self-esteem is no longer based primarily on unconditional acceptance but on what we merit from our sustained contributions. Thus in the whole of our life there is a tension between earning approval and receiving it as a free gift of love. The infinite variation of this tension is the dramatic arena of our life. This conflict is at the root of the division of Christendom between the Reformers and the Catholic tradition. The Reformers believed in justification by faith; in other words, we cannot do anything to merit our salvation, it is a gift from God which we receive from faith. The image of man, in this theology, is fallen humanity that can do nothing to redeem itself. It is a fallen world rescued by Christ from its badness.

Man has no pristine integrity but is rescued from his innate badness. Catholicism accepts man's fall and Christ's rescue but makes allowances for man's attempt to achieve goodness through his own efforts. Thus in the tension between these two divisions of Christianity, the psychological roots of unconditional love and that earned by effort feature in theological terms.

Our self-esteem is dependent in another way on others, this time in terms of our freedom in relating. As young children we approach our parents, relatives and friends with an absolute certainty of our welcomed acceptance. We may be shy but we do not readily entertain the possibility of not being wanted. This feeling begins to emerge in some people in adolescence and then in adult life. The feeling may be conscious or unconscious and the implications are considerable. If conscious, we feel bad, ugly, unattractive, undesired, unwanted and cannot believe that anybody wants us. Sometimes, as previously mentioned, the consequences are that we choose a friend or spouse who is actually critical, disparaging and fulfils our need to be criticised. In these circumstances our freedom to seek what we really want – namely unconditional loving – is seriously restricted. We select those who actually destroy us and it may take a very long time to discover what we are doing to ourselves; something which contributes to marital breakdown.

If our self-rejection is unconscious we may become afraid to seek intimate relationships or intimacy. We are afraid of both these experiences and we do not know why. We are not conscious of the fact that deep in ourselves we feel no good and we are afraid that, as others get closer to us, they will discover the undesirable bits of ourselves and ultimately reject us. In these circumstances we are always hiding from ourselves because we are afraid to discover that which we dread deep inside us.

Poor self-esteem and the rejection of ourselves need not be a permanent phenomenon in our lives, although it is in a number of people. Self-esteem can fluctuate with our mood. When we are low and depressed we do not like ourselves and find it difficult to let others approach us. These feelings are transient but are crucial when people are depressed because self-rejection and hate are at their extreme and are associated with the desire for self-destruction and suicide. These are situations in which people become slaves to meaninglessness. They feel they are worthless, have nothing to give and deserve little other than rejection. We can only reassure such people by our constant and unconditional love and, of course, the appropriate medical intervention when needed.

Anger – Guilt – Reparation

Perhaps one of the commonest sources of the feelings of badness is our anger and its consequences. Before I describe these, it is worth diverting for a moment to a fundamental psychological controversy. It was Freud and his successors who maintained that aggression is a basic human instinct with which we all arrive in this world. It is part of our make-up and we cannot escape from its consequences. Such a view of man makes conflict, war and destruction inevitable and it gives a pessimistic view of the future of civilisation. Some of Freud's successors, however, have maintained that we do not inherit a biological instinct of aggression. Instead, aggression is seen as a response to the environment. If the environment is not threatening we do not need to resort to aggression. In this view, social conditions can produce a society which is just, fair, equal and one which minimises the need for aggressive responses. At the present moment we have no way of deciding this issue definitely. The argument has profound implications. If aggression is innate, then we can only modify it; if it is a response to situations, we can ultimately change the situations permanently. At present the evidence supports a mixture of both views, but in practice we all have to cope with our aggression and its consequences.

Freud traces aggression to the first year of life; Melanie Klein to the first few months. In both instances the child develops teeth, bites the breast, causes pain and a withdrawal reaction by mother. Gradually its nails scratch and, little by little, it learns to scream, kick, bite, use its fists and so on in physical violence. Little by little, physical violence is converted to verbal and emotional violence but, at its most elementary form, it returns to its physical character.

The immediate reaction to aggression and the causation of

pain to others, particularly those who are close to us, is a feeling of guilt. This is an emotion of discomfort, at times acute in its intensity, coupled with a number of other features. First we cannot take back our aggression and therefore we are prisoners of our action and at the mercy of our victim. We feel temporarily helpless, and as young children we felt very much at the mercy of our parents, teachers and our elders. Guilt is mixed with the fear of retaliation, punishment or humiliation.

But how do we deal with guilt without being destroyed by it? The answer is that we want forgiveness and want to make reparation. Thus aggression has a series of consequences which can be consistent with human integrity or not. Aggression, damage, reparation and forgiveness are the patterns of integrity; aggression, guilt, humiliation and non-forgiveness the patterns of distortion. These patterns play an enormous part in our adult life. All close adult relationships have the capacity to trigger off aggression, physical, verbal, emotional, or a combination of two or more. Normally the person who transgresses feels regret and guilt, seeks forgiveness, is forgiven and does adequate reparation. But each one of these stages can present difficulties depending on earlier childhood experiences.

Some people have been made to feel so bad and their guilt is so excessive that they cannot believe they are ever going to be forgiven and enter into a state of despair. Such excessive guilt may lead to endless and excessive reparation. Forgiveness too may have been associated with humiliating punishment which has left such a mark that a person finds it impossible to apologise later on in life. One hears again and again in marital difficulties of the spouse who never apologises and always expects their partner to make the first sign of reconciliation. Such people are judged severely but, when one looks at their background, one finds that they are so terrified of contrition, so terrified of being in the wrong that they cannot take the necessary steps. They are afraid that saying sorry means becoming small, helpless children and their freedom to accept responsibility for their deeds is severely restricted. Then there are those who find it very difficult to forgive. If criticised or hurt, they go into a long period of sulking and withdrawal which may last for days and weeks. They punish their aggression by withdrawing their availability for inordinately long periods and even then they never forgive completely; or, if they do, they remind their spouse or friend of their misdeeds for years afterwards. In fact there are men and women who never forgive or forget a hurt and never remember a positive or loving act. Their receptivity is channelled to being rejected and that is the only experience which is registered.

The cycle of hurt, guilt, forgiveness and reparation is fundamental in human relationships and in the man-God encounter. Without feelings of guilt, humanity is brutalised; without forgiveness and compassion, the consequences can be lethal. The ultimate value proposed to us comes from Christ who invites us to forgive – not only our friends but our enemies: to forgive, not once but seventy times seven and not only to forgive but to turn the other cheek. Only divine love can accomplish these virtues, but we are beckoned to imitate and this is an invitation we can respond to daily in our life.

Ambivalence

I mention love because love and anger towards the same person is closely allied to aggression and is another fundamental human condition that we have constantly to negotiate.

Ambivalence, which denotes mixed feelings towards the same person, enters our life very early on. The mother who appears to be all loving, suddenly says 'No' in a harsh tone, in due course smacks us, later punishes us in other ways. Very soon we have to learn that the significant other, who is all loving, can also be the source of pain, hurt, criticism and rejection. Having mixed feelings for another person can torture us. We love and are also angry. We trust and have doubts. We rely and are dubious. Ultimately we can love and hate the same person. The world's most poignant tragedies have been written with this theme in mind. In fact this is a challenge of constant integrity for our own feelings towards ourselves and those close to us. Love and rejection, trust and mistrust, reliance and incompetence in ourselves and the same feelings in others govern so much of our life. We are longing for absolute integrity in which the positive triumphs over the negative, but such absoluteness is rare. Sometimes we strive with heavy odds against us. For one reason or another our capacity to cope with frustration may be limited, the speed with which we explode is excessive, the damage we do is constant and severe. If we are handicapped in this way with excessive irritability our freedom is curtailed, but in normal circumstances there is an unceasing battle in which integrity involves our loving and positive feelings being always in the ascendancy and greater than our hate and destruction.

In this chapter I have described some of our fundamental feelings and emotions which start in infancy and childhood, are shaped by our life then, and continue to play crucial roles in later life. We are constantly aiming to achieve integrity within the limits of freedom that our constitution and upbringing have given us, within the wider possibilities of the society we live in. This society enters our life when we enter school, the world of our peers, sexual relationships, friendship, marriage, the single state: and these are the states I will examine next.

8

Freedom and Integrity II

School

The early years of our life condition us to the experiences of love, mediated through the body, through signals of feeling recognised, wanted and appreciated; in brief, through unconditional loving. It is true that we have to comply with the demands of our parents but these do not appear excessive and the sense of being lovable is acquired in intimate personal relationships between ourselves and our parents. Above all, at this stage in life, we do not have to earn our love.

When we go to school a different situation arises. We are no longer simply precious persons in the eyes of our parents. We are members of a new community called the school. There we gradually learn to acquire a social role. Now we are pupils and our status is assessed in relationship to the other pupils and teachers. In our primary school allowances are still made for our youth but less so. We are increasingly assessed by our competence and willingness to fit in with the school requirements. Our value is now gradually assessed on our performance and our goodness or badness on our achievements. Above all, there is now entering in our life the first awareness of qualification by results. We are praised for our accomplishments, our status is based on a comparison with others and our self-esteem dependent on our talents. School brings us in touch with a world that is always to be with us; a world that does not appreciate primarily our lovability but our competence and so justification by results becomes both a freedom and a constraint. In theory we are free to reach the highest achievements; in practice we have to accept in the course of our life something much lower. Our image of ourselves is going to be a composite of self-esteem, based on being loved and on our achievements, and we shall struggle between the two until our death.

School not only opens the gates of achievement and competition, it also introduces us to other human beings with whom we have to relate. We will gradually have to assume a social role. Some of the other children may become our friends; most will not. Thus, with the majority of the other pupils we have to develop a new form of relationship and this is based on justice. We transact our relationships on what is fair, just and equitable. Our integrity now depends on not sing nor exploiting others. Social transactions have to be just and depend on giving and receiving goods and services which are equitable. Just as love is the key to personal intimacy, so justice is the medium of interpersonal exchange.

How free we are to be and act justly depends on the integrity of the society we live in and the integrity of our motives. From our schooldays we are tempted to exploit the weak, the helpless, the innocent; indeed all those who put themselves in our power: and that is precisely what we must not do.

Adolescence

This sense of justice expands in its range of possibilities as we grow older and covers our adolescence. Unlike the love we experience from our family, we realise increasingly that society owes nothing to us except the rewards of labour, the protection it offers to all citizens, and social welfare. Adolescence is also a private time when we are trying to disengage from our parents and therefore we experience a wide range of loneliness. We are physically, socially and emotionally alone. This aloneness can compromise both our freedom and our integrity.

Our freedom depends on the fact that we have to be attractive enough to engage the attention of others. We may have a high self-esteem but usually this is a period of uncertainty and doubt about ourselves. Our childhood is receding but we have not yet become adults. We are in an in-between phase. In this in-between phase we turn to our peers for companionship, self discovery, leadership and the discovery of adolescent values. Adolescents form groups in which they escape on the one hand from childhood and on the other from adulthood. These groupings are transient even though some members become lifelong friends.

Within these groups we can lose our independence. Instead of evaluating life through our own judgments, we rely on the leader who becomes a parental substitute. We pay attention to detail almost in a ritualistic manner. Our freedom is constrained by the need to conform and imitate. We can temporarily lose our identity in the midst of others. This loss and confusion can go on in adult life when we dread parties and social gatherings, which terrify us as we gradually feel we lose the sense of ourselves in the midst of others.

We may find separation from parents so difficult that we are unable to assert our independence and to give up our dependence on our parents. Some youngsters refuse to budge from their parental dependence and cannot leave home. They are however caught in a trap. They want to move forward, which frightens them, and they resent their dependence at home, which makes them angry. Such young men and women are truly removed from their integrity. This ambivalence can continue in life. Such men and women may try to solve their problem by marrying strong, decisive and authoritarian spouses. The ambivalence however continues. They want to lean on their partners for support and they resent feeling trapped as emotional prisoners. Such marriages are full of conflict.

But the ordinary adolescent moves in and out of groups, gets what he/she needs and then continues this pattern of behaviour until a new intimate relationship emerges in which they can find the sense of being recognised for their uniqueness, wanted for their characteristics and loved for themselves.

Adolescent Sexuality

Part of this twosome intimacy is sexual and sexuality plays a big role in adolescence. This is the time when the body, acquainted with physical contact as an expression of affection, has to integrate the newly awakened erotic and genital dimension. Ultimately, the affectionate and erotic encounters have to fuse and this is the supreme achievement of wholesome love, but of course there are difficulties.

The emerging adolescent may have been warned off or forbidden to indulge in sexual pleasure. Very often he or she ignores this and masturbates but with a marked sense of guilt. Often the adolescent has been told little, if anything, and masturbation is carried out in an inner atmosphere of unease and guilt. In my own opinion, this is the time when the adolescent has to find out about their sexual body with both freedom and integrity and masturbation is one expression of this. It is a temporary phenomenon because the sexual drive seeks another person to really express itself and so the boy-girl relationship emerges. This relationship is a prelude to friendship, courtship and normally marriage.

If we remember that some young people find it very difficult to get close to the opposite sex, or feel low in their self-esteem or do not really believe anybody would want them, then the evolving heterosexual intimacy will not occur. Such men and women remain isolated and feel too shy to mix. Sexually, they can continue masturbating and having transient affairs or even living together as a way of overcoming their doubts about themselves. An ultimate loss of integrity is the prostitute and her client. The man needs sexual relief but cannot get close to a woman emotionally. The visit to the prostitute bypasses his problem. For a fee he gets sex without personal involvement.

But of course all couples who live together prior to marriage are not that disturbed. Basically, these men and women need their freedom and are afraid of commitment, although they want intimacy. So they compromise. They live together and have closeness; they make love and have sex; but they remain free of the commitment to permanency and children. Their integrity is compromised at the level of continuity and reliability. They cannot offer the vision of continuity because they have not acquired the freedom of permanency. They do not feel reliable within themselves and cannot risk either permanency or procreation. They are not emotionally free to make themselves fully available and so they compromise. This compromise may be the only available course of action to them but it is a compromise and should be considered as such.

In this compromise, sexual intercourse is freely shared.

Yet there is a long and deep tradition against premarital intercourse. This is not simply a Christian killer of pleasure. Both humanity and Christianity claim that premarital abstention from intercourse is possible and consistent with human integrity. At the very heart of this argument is the belief that sexual intercourse is not the appropriate means of discovering the authenticity of a relationship. Sex is a body language and its most simple characteristics are physical penetration genitally which ultimately gives an exquisite pleasure. But this pleasure tells us nothing about the person behind it. Sexual intercourse cannot be the basis of exploring the nature of the other person. Only intimacy and self disclosure can do this in friendship. Only when these are established and the couple wish to transform the friendship into a permanent commitment does sex play its important part. Sexual intercourse seals and completes the personal encounter; it is a very blunt instrument for establishing authentic relationship. Many couples anticipate sex before they get married. Although, strictly speaking, this is short of full integrity, it is much nearer a presentation of authentic human relationship than casual sex.

There are however the Don Juans of this world who have an incessant need for sex quite independently of a personal relationship. Until recently we thought of the promiscuous as relentless pursuers of pleasure. There is scientific evidence that this is not always the case. Men and women who are extroverts need a lot of sensation in order to be stimulated. They need a lot of activity, a great deal of involvement, a lot of action and a great deal of sex. For them, sex is often a mechanical experience but it is needed by such a person as part of the general excitement in their life. We all know people who crave for excitement but are shallow and incapable of retaining experiences. Experiences appear to last for a short period and the need for further stimulation becomes imperative. Promiscuous men and women fall into this category and need much greater understanding and sympathy.

Courtship
In the later stages of adolescence most couples enter the world of courtship with the idea of getting married. This is a normal

phenomenon. I want to draw attention, however, to the type of courtship leading to marriage which is not a process reflecting the freedom of the couple. Some people are in such distress at home that they are longing to get away. Such homes may be filled with overt discord and much quarrelling. The girl or boy may feel unwanted, rejected; or feels that another brother or sister is preferred. The motive for court- ship, living together or marrying is not a free choice of these states but the desire to escape from intolerant situations. Thus the option of marriage is not freely chosen but rushed into as an alternative to an intolerable situation at home. Another lack of freedom is the girl or boy who drifts into marriage because it is the cultural thing to do. Early marriage is a phenomenon of the lower socio-economic group. After school such people marry because no alternative is so acceptable.

Another reason for drifting into marriage for many people, particularly for women, is the fact that engagement and marriage give the individual a social status, meaning and purpose which work does not. A ring on the left hand is a symbol of having arrived at a socially recognised point. It gives status, role, and lifts the person from meaninglessness.

But all these reasons augur badly for the marriage. Gradu- ally people get their self-confidence and sense of worth inde- pendently of the marriage and find they are trapped in an institution for life with someone who may mean less and less to them with the passage of time. Life gives these people what marriage is supposed to have granted and marriage with this particular spouse may become pointless.

Marriage
But of course for the majority of couples who marry in their mid-twenties, marriage is loaded with meaning. Contem- porary marriage with its openness, equality of relationship between the spouses and full communication allows the couple an emotional intimacy which is strongly reminiscent of the first intimate relationship between child and parent.

Dependence
If this is the case, then integrity within marriage has to safeguard several dimensions of the personality. The couple

return to a state of wanting to be recognised, wanted and appreciated unconditionally. This is rarely possible but many couples mix unconditional acceptance with an exchange practice, i.e. they love each other without thinking about the cost and also expect an exchange of goods, services and help from each other.

In treating each other in this way, there are a number of emotional experiences which couples have to work out. The first is dependence. Unconditional loving is linked with dependence. Not only do we want to be loved but also to be able to depend on our spouse. This mutual dependence is natural and expresses integrity. But dependence can be misinterpreted. We can continue to rely on our spouse as a parent. On the surface such a relationship appears admirable. But there are two forms of dependence. There is one form in which we depend on our spouse physically, socially and emotionally. But if this reliability is for some reason withdrawn temporarily or not available, the mature authentic person does not disintegrate. They can survive temporarily without their spouse who is absent, sick or incapable. The other form of dependence is on the surface similar but, if the support is withdrawn temporarily, the other person collapses. Their dependence was complete and infantile. Removal of support means removal of a life-giving channel. Such people are, of course, not free in their loving, which is conditioned by their fear of losing the one they depend on totally.

Intimacy

Another dimension which is significant in marriage is that of closeness and distance. At the very heart of an intimate relationship – such as marriage – closeness features conspicuously. This closeness may be physical, social, intellectual, spiritual or emotional. The married couple want to be close to each other physically, participate in social activity together, share the same values and ideas and express their oneness sexually and through affection. All this is normal and natural. But each partner also needs his/her space, freedom, room to be a private human being. Most couples achieve this balance of closeness and distance satisfactorily. But there are couples where one spouse needs greater closeness than the other. This is interpreted as clinging by the other spouse who is constantly trying to escape from the suffocation of an excessive and demanding closeness. The clinging partner may be afraid of being abandoned, may find isolation intolerable or may need a great deal of demonstration of affection. Freedom and integrity require a balance of togetherness and separateness. Some people escape from the suffocation by having an affair or ultimately leaving altogether. The person who needs closeness may appear to be constantly nagging. Both need help to adjust to their mutual requirements.

Trust

A third dimension is trust. Ordinarily couples trust each other's intentions, the uttered and the silent, the professed and the latent. Such trust is a basic freedom and integrity for loving. To profess to love and not mean it is, of course, a massive repudiation of integrity. Sometimes love gradually wanes in marriage and is replaced by habit. Habit is the expression of routine in which the external proceeds without internal validation. Love becomes diluted to a point where it no longer exists and duty has taken its place. When one loves and the other returns a social convention, the sense of feeling unwanted can be profound.

The sense of feeling unwanted can also occur at any time in the long relationship of marriage in the presence of morbid jealousy. The jealous person expects to be displaced by a third party and the threat is so massive that phantasy takes over. Spouses are attacked for having affairs that do not exist. No reassurance can erase the suspicion which dominates the inner world of the jealous person and creates havoc. The integrity of the relationship suffers and can lead to the dissolution of the marriage. The jealous person has very little emotional freedom to trust and they are prisoners of their anxious and insecure make-up.

Communication

An essential component for sorting out all these dimensions is communication. We communicate with words and actions. Most couples need both. They need to talk to each other and they need to see the evidence of love in action, by doing to and for each other things that please. Some people are better at doing than talking. They are the practical-orientated handymen who repair, look after the garden, construct necessary bits in the house; and there are, unfortunately, those whose only skill with a hammer is to damage themselves or who are such perfectionists that any job takes years instead of days.

It is however in dialogue that freedom and integrity are much in advance. Freedom here often means the absence of fear which allows each spouse to say to each other the full truth of how they feel, what they want and what they are planning. Fear which suppresses communication can be devastating. It is invariably acted out in painful actions. People get drunk and then say all the nasty things they have suppressed. They become irritable and lose their temper for no reason, with outbursts that are triggered off by trivia. They say and do things which are highly aggressive when their pent-up fury is disgorged. The loss of freedom through fear of aggression or punishment in adults can be devastating.

When a dialogue does take place, integrity requires that we listen not only to words and reason but to the feelings behind the words; that we listen carefully and do not simply wait for the other person to stop in order for us to start. We need not only to listen but to be open to the truth of what the other is saying, otherwise we simply listen to criticise or condemn.

We also communicate with our bodies. We can look mystified, unbelieving, dubious, mistrusting or dismissive. We can use our arms and legs to show impatience, incredulity and disbelief. We can look at our spouse or at the floor or the ceiling. We can turn our bodies away from them or get close in a menacing, angry manner. Ultimately we can strike physically.

All this means that our fear or anger have markedly reduced our freedom, capacity to accept responsibility, or freedom to see the truth and change. We may be terrified of changing or losing control and being helpless children.

Lack of integrity is also seen in sexual intercourse. We may be making love but totally disengaged from our partner as the object of our love. We may be simply interested in the mechanics of sex with no appreciation of the body or person of our lover. We may be making love to our spouse and phantasising the presence of somebody else or our spouse behaving in a totally different way. Integrity requires the fusion of the physical and emotional within the same person with whom we are engaged in intercourse. Planning next week's menu whilst having sex is not an authentic exchange.

The Single State

Of course all the expression of loving is not limited to the married. Single people have a great deal of affinity with the married. They too want unconditional loving and also loving based on the exchange of ideas, values and services. Their principal source of affection is friendship and their special relationship with God. If their single state is to have integrity it must be chosen deliberately and not drifted into out of fear of closeness in marriage or fear of sex. Some single people have opted out of intimacy or sex out of fear and these men and women have to grow and mature as have the married. Such growth can occur through friendship, prayer and the life of the community they belong to, be it the parish or religious life.

At the heart of the integrity of the single person is to have chosen or accepted the state because they want to make their availability a gift to others. They want to meet others without the restrictions of the married life. That means they have to grow in self-esteem and sense of power to reach and love others. Growth in self-esteem through which love is given to others is the key feature of the single person.

The married grow in self-esteem through affectionate intimacy and sexual intercourse. What about the single? Affectionate intimacy in friendship is essential for the single person and the isolated life of withdrawal is an active handicap, to be gradually removed. What about sex? This is the point of the greatest difference between Christian and non-Christian. The latter sees sex as a need, a game, an outlet, and considers it appropriate to seek it from any source that is available. The Christian has no less need for physical sex. Sex is a good experience and its avoidance is not on the grounds that pleasure is evil. Its avoidance is based on the grounds that sex and person form one fused entity and, in indulging in the one, there is a human necessity to recognise and respect the other. This is what the single person gives up, sex as a pleasure and as an encounter with another person that requires a continuing relationship.

Giving up sex does not mean ceasing to be a sexual person. One dresses, relates, acts, feels and relates as a sexual person. Giving up sex does not mean giving up physical encounter. Long before puberty we touched, held and hugged and kissed our parents, brothers and sisters and friends as an expression of non-erotic intimacy. The single person needs all this non-erotic physical closeness and need not be afraid of it.

Ultimately, what about the need for physical sex? This too does not disappear in the single person. It is gradually brought under control, in some people much more easily than in others. Thus single people will occasionally have spontaneous orgasms, will want to masturbate or even have intercourse. We know that the struggle for sexual containment does not succeed overnight. All these sexual activities may occur from time to time and their presence is not an absolute contra-indication to the single state. Gradually the urge will subside, even if it takes a long time. Provided the commitment of generosity to serve others remains, sexual lapses do not matter. If the single person, however, recognises a clear and powerful sexual drive, then further consideration should be given as to the suitability of the single state.

What about the single person who is so involuntarily, who does not want to be single and, indeed, has sexual relations with men and women in a loving setting? There are these confused states and it is vital that the person examines their motives, feelings, fears and needs. Integrity requires that marriage or the single state be embraced for its unique qualities and not as a compromise or escape. There are plenty of compromises and escapes but the aim of being human is to acquire the freedom to pursue either state with integrity.

In conclusion it can be seen that human relationships are constrained by the social conditions of a particular society, within which the individual characteristics of the person restrains or facilitates the fullness of the realisation of the human potential latent in the individual or the couple. There is no stage or state in life that commands absolute freedom and integrity. There is a journey we all undertake which requires vigilance, effort, commitment, suffering and the occasional triumph. Both suffering and triumphs are the peaks of glancing the image of God we reflect, but Christ's freedom and integrity remain the constant signs for the whole of our journey, which is only concluded in the freedom and integrity we share with the living in the world to come. In this world we get gradual glimpses of both but the invitation to persist is found in our Lord Jesus Christ, whose own life reveals both the dimensions in full and who never ceases to invite us to be as perfect as our heavenly Father.

9

The Meaning of Suffering

The Pain of Existence
Suffering is one of the most frequent experiences of daily life
and one which constantly prompts the question as to its
meaning and purpose. Indeed those who wish to attack the
idea of God challenge theists with the paradox that a God
who is all-loving nevertheless lives with and permits so much
suffering in the world. How are the two to be reconciled?

The presence of severe mental and physical handicap, the
sudden transition from normality to ill-health, the pain of
loss, the ultimate tragedy of death are constant reminders
that suffering is never far away. Suffering seems to be even
more inexplicable when a young person with special gifts is
struck down with some disabling disease or dies. What can
one say when a gifted child is struck with malignant disease
before its talents have matured?

In all these circumstances we are faced with a mystery. It
is a mystery which some consider negates the idea of a source
of all goodness, and therefore of the divine, as the origin and
meaning of life. Such people contend that if God existed he
would have arranged things better and there would not be
such a waste of human effort and endeavour. For them, God
and suffering are incompatible concepts and the reality of the
latter precludes the former. The alternative to the theory of
divine origin is that of evolution brought about by the blind
forces of chance. But suffering is only too patently part of
such a system. Evolution, in all its stages, implies the disap-
pearance of some species and the survival of others, and the
disappearing groups experience pain, suffering and ultimately
defeat. An evolutionary philosophy of life does not eliminate

suffering, but, says the atheist, it does at least remove the absurdity of an all-loving God.

It will be argued here that love and suffering are not incompatible, that they are in fact mutually dependent, and that a God of love who permits suffering is thus not an absurdity. At the very centre of love there is a need to overcome everything that resists it. Resistance has been variously interpreted as the presence of evil, sin, demons and malign powers and suffering is one essential way of overcoming this resistance.

Social Suffering

When we talk or write about suffering we think primarily of personal suffering, but we are becoming increasingly aware nowadays of social suffering. This change of emphasis from private to public, from the life of the individual to that of the community, has been a welcome change in direction. In the recent past religion and faith were primarily concerned with the salvation of the individual's own soul. Salvation was seen in terms of the person in isolation from his/her neighbour. Today we recognise increasingly that both our faith and our salvation are communal phenomena, and the Church is described as the people of God. What happens to any members of the human race, and in particular to any of the people of God anywhere, involves all of us. The sufferings of others is our suffering also. Psychologically this is very difficult because suffering is part of our affective life and is restricted by the bonds of affectivity which operate in our love for ourselves and the feelings we have for those with whom we are in relationship. Thus our distant or overseas neighbour who is not closely linked with us is not somebody who can easily arouse feelings of concern in us. Nevertheless it is one of the most optimistic signs of the times that our concern does extend beyond our immediate world, that our experience of personal suffering is added to that of social suffering which can relate to our own or to an outside community.

But it is our personal suffering that we are most aware of and it is this that we have to consider next. Perhaps the most basic form of suffering is pain in our body. Physical pain can be excruciating and a great deal of modern research has been devoted to its elimination. Indeed modern medicine has made so much progress that persistent severe pain need no longer be a part of the human condition, at least among the developed nations. But minor discomfort is never far away from us and it is a constant reminder that although man has conquered space he has certainly not conquered physical ailment.

After physical pain there is the suffering that arises in our daily life as it brings us into contact with others. Our social integrity is an essential part of our identity. At work, in our leisure activities, at church, in the community, we are identified as people of worth through our social standing. If we become unemployed, if we are dismissed from work or fail to get the position we think we deserve, we are distressed. If we are excluded from our social club, excommunicated from the life of the Church or disgraced in the community, we go through the agony of public and spiritual disgrace.

Finally we experience mental anguish. Nobody escapes the distress of anxiety, for example. We worry about our survival and the survival of those we love. We are concerned with our well-being and that of those for whom we care. Some people experience marked anxiety which may take the form of constant worry or phobias about people and situations. Take the question of mood. Most of us go through phases of exceptional well-being or misery, which we call elation or depression. For most people these are transient phenomena which colour the mood, but we know that depressive reactions are common and in their midst there is physical and emotional upheaval, with a change of inner direction towards hopelessness and despair. Ultimately the depressed person finds no comfort in man or God, despairs, and yearns to terminate a life of agony, and many do.

Anxiety and depression are the commonest mental disturbances leading to severe illnesses, but they are not the only ones. More rarely there are the men and women who suffer from what have come to be known as the schizophrenic illnesses where thought disorder, delusions and hallucinations are present. Here there is temporarily a grave loss of mental functioning with disorganisation of the personality.

Other Factors

Mental illness, however, is not the only form of disturbance that can bring people to the verge of despair. Young people who find their life temporarily meaningless take refuge in drugs. Men and women who find it difficult to cope resort to alcohol which, like drugs, can become an addiction. The break-up of a marriage, the loss of a loved one, the chaos of business loss, can all have calamitous effects with much distress and suffering. The question to which we return repeatedly is: what is the meaning of it all?

Not all suffering is meaningless. At the personal level we can begin to detect some purpose in suffering as a warning system for our survival. Let us take the simple example of physical pain. A pain in the abdomen can be the warning sign of an inflamed appendix or a peptic ulcer, of gallstones, kidney stones and many other conditions. Some of these conditions need surgical intervention if life is to be saved; others need surgical intervention for the elimination of a diseased organ, the simplest instance being toothache. But even before the advent of modern medicine, pain was a warning that the body needed rest and time to repair its resources. In some circumstances, therefore, physical pain is an effective warning system, essential for the survival of the body. But unfortunately this is not always the case; there is also chronic pain, as in rheumatoid arthritis or the terminal stages of cancer, which is an expression of irreversible tissue damage that is no longer subject to therapeutic intervention. Diseases such as disseminated sclerosis and other nervous and muscular conditions cause progressive, irreparable and often devastating harm. Nevertheless there is no doubt that a great deal of physical pain has a warning value which is beneficial to the whole person.

Let us also look at another common manifestation, which is that of anxiety. All of us are familiar with the sensations of anxiety. We become aware of a sense of discomfort, irritability, even a sense of danger, and in these circumstances we want to take action to reverse the situation. Animals are prone to anxiety and for them this is a particularly useful warning signal; in its presence they can 'freeze', stay put and fight or run away. We also do these things. Often when we become aware of anxiety, either we stop and take stock of the situation, or we run away from the site of danger, or else, if we have no alternative, we fight for our survival. All these are healthy responses and they have a survival value. But we also know that anxiety can become a way of life. People can become over-anxious and worry about the least little thing; their anxiety can grow to such proportions that it becomes a disease and it has really no survival value. Once again suffering becomes meaningless; not only meaningless but also destructive, as when aggression takes over human beings and becomes the way of settling disputes. Some of the most painful moments in the history of Christianity are those in which Christians have taken up arms against each other. Thus even here, in the case of aggression, that which has survival value can be removed from its context and become something awesome and destructive. This is amply illustrated in the weapons of war we now possess whose capacity for devastation is far removed from the essential function of aggression, which is to ensure survival with minimum damage. Most species of animals display all the signs of aggressivity, but they are in fact expert at achieving their end with the minimum spilling of blood. Human beings have not imitated them and now have weapons capable of such devastation that the survival of life itself will be threatened.

One of the points to emerge so far, therefore, is that some suffering has survival value whilst some has not; that some suffering should be eliminated, but some should not; that some suffering is creative and some is destructive. But which suffering is acceptable and which is not, and how can we distinguish between the two?

This is a crucial question in all our lives. We can begin to see that not all suffering is purposeless.

Human Concern

At the international level everyone agrees that we should not let people perish as a result of famine, exposure to cold and heat, poor sanitation, floods, earthquakes and similar devastation: that we must recognise the important principle that people should not suffer when they are helpless victims of natural disaster. But we have gone further and we try to protect the innocent victims of war or other adverse circumstances, having ceased to interpret these events as divine acts of retribution for which people deserve to suffer. We owe it to them to relieve their suffering – so much has become clear – and our doing so is a good example of suffering being conquered by human concern, which can broadly be called love.

At the national level societies are increasingly shifting to a situation in which the poor in their midst also have their suffering alleviated. An obvious example of this is the fact that those who fall below a certain level of poverty are picked up and supported by the state. Everyone is entitled to a minimum of health care and educational support and under this umbrella some receive a great deal from the state. Once again we see here a raising of the level of awareness of what is tolerable in terms of human suffering and of when we expect the state to intervene. There are other reliefs which are emerging in society. In the past the imprisoned, the divorced, or the homosexual experienced excessive social suffering in consequence of their behaviour. But society is beginning to realise here also that a number of these people are in fact victims of personal circumstances and that they endure enough in their predicament without having to undergo any further suffering.

Some people would dispute the benefit of what I have been describing. They see the intervention of the state as an intrusion into what should be the field of private effort and any initiative of public forgiveness as an insidious form of permissiveness. They would wish to restore the penalties of material and social suffering as a means of controlling behaviour, and this view prevailed for a long time. Today we are coming to realise that adding the scourge of guilt in relation to public behaviour is not a constructive way of using suffering.

Disease Form
In the world of psychiatry we make a further distinction between constructive and destructive suffering. As I have mentioned already, we all experience anxiety and depression, but in some people these conditions become illnesses. Every psychiatrist has to learn to distinguish between variants of

98

normal anxiety and depression and their disease form. The former are in fact a means of coping with life and can be creative; the latter have outstripped their usefulness and are utterly destructive, to the point of suicide in the case of depression. In their disease form these conditions have to be relieved by appropriate treatment, whereas anxiety and depression in their own forms have to be used effectively in life with the help of counselling.

At times psychiatrists are not able to relieve suffering because of the person's insistence that God wants him to suffer. This is particularly true in depression, where he feels that he deserves to suffer because of his misdeeds – which, often enough, are an expression of the illness. When treatment is allowed and the depression is cleared, a totally different approach can be taken and it becomes clear that God does not want this particular distress.

Just as some people decry the relief of social adversity, so others are critical of psychological help, particularly in depression. This criticism is valid up to a point. It has been shown that both these experiences have their uses and that their early and instant removal is not always conducive to growth. In the same way that a very young child cannot be indefinitely protected if he has to learn that fire burns, so the elimination of all anxiety and depression would leave people psychologically unprepared to recognise warning signals of these conditions.

We are now reaching a stage where we can refer to the possibility of suffering as being creative, and this needs examination.

10

Suffering and Relationship

Maintaining a Relationship
One of the elements of suffering in our society is isolation.
We take it for granted that every human being can form
associations, friendships and intimate loving relationships.
This is not the case. There are men and women who are
isolated because they have lost their spouse, their children
have left them, they have grown old, are sick or disabled.
These are social reasons for loneliness and a caring
community should be able to overcome them.

The real suffering occurs in those who are physically
healthy but emotionally damaged and who cannot get close
to others. Often these men and women do not know or understand why they are lonely. Close examination reveals that
intimacy puts them into a state of panic. They may or may
not be conscious of the fear which keeps them away from
other people, but the panic is caused by the feeling that others
do not find them attractive or good enough and that, when
they get to know them, they are bound to reject them. Even
when they feel welcomed they find it difficult to register and
maintain affection. They cannot really believe that they are
wanted or appreciated. Their degree of mistrust is so high
that the slightest error on the part of those befriending them
is interpreted as an attack or rejection and they withdraw.

These are the loners of this world, and in this pool of lonely
people we find the alcoholics, drug addicts, many who visit
prostitutes or lead promiscuous lives, all trying to drown their
aloneness with transient gratification. Others withdraw into
themselves and pursue solitary lives.

In the past these men and women were integrated in the
extended family network or a social structure which had room

for everyone. Today these supportive structures are no longer available. The pub often becomes the solace of the solitary man who cannot relate but needs the comfort of the presence of others. A few use their handicap to challenge the oceans as single-handed sailors, or climb mountains. Whatever the individual solution, in the depths of such a person there is a pain of the absence, recognised or unrecognised, of the stimulus of human interaction. Finally the loner becomes mentally ill and it is to the psychiatrist that lonely people turn in great numbers when their isolation overwhelms them. In this predicament, either people can be rescued from the grim reality of being alone, or they become susceptible to suicide which they see as the final solution to their desolation. Every day a thousand people kill themselves the world over, and this is probably a conservative estimate. The coroner's courts witness daily the effects of the cruel suffering of isolation.

We all come across these people continually, and if our love for God can be translated into love of neighbour, then the pastoral challenge is to try to form a relationship with one such person. If each of us could accept the responsibility for a single act of rescue, then we would become the good Samaritan in an area where the needs are great and the labourers too few.

The majority of human beings can form relationships. We go through the stages of finding out whether we share a common background, attitudes, opinions, values and so forth, and proceed from this social testing to a personal one — whether we feel acknowledged, wanted and appreciated. There can be much agonising in this process of personal interaction. Each member of the dyad is anxious as to whether or not he/she will be accepted by the other. To receive the love of another human being is a precious happening over which we have no control. It is a gift we cannot command, and as we wait in uncertainty we go through a series of private crucifixions. We live between the certainty of desire and the uncertainty of the other's response.

Sometimes this agony is prolonged when our lover is uncertain of his/her feelings, or at times when we ourselves hesitate in our response. Normally it is the trepidation of being rejected which concerns us. Will we be wanted or not? The question whether we are going to be accepted or rejected fills our whole inner world. Years later we shall put individual attempts to form a relationship into perspective, but while it is happening our whole being is taken up with what the outcome of the exchange will be. We are shot from grief to elation and back to despair. What is at stake at the moment of the formation of a relationship is the very survival of the meaning of our being. We offer the whole of ourselves and await the outcome. This experience of falling in love happens more often when we are young but it recurs throughout our lives. Indeed, even when two people have accepted each other, the challenge of love is to maintain the initial splendour of the experience.

Under Attack

As we become intimate with another human being, enduring love is tested by frequent interjections of criticism and conflict. Love and anger are the opposite sides of the same coin. Love can only survive if the attacks we receive and launch do not ultimately destroy our trust in each other.

A certain amount of criticism is common in any relationship and inevitable in a close intimate one. We do things that upset the other and the list of irritations can be long. The annoyance begins to assume seriousness when it accumulates, deepens and becomes bitter. Perhaps the commonest criticism that we experience from those close to us is that we are selfish. We are attacked because we are thought to put ourselves first, to think only of our own needs, to be imperceptive or insensitive of the other, to be lazy or unconcerned. The grounds for our apparent selfishness are endless and depend on the way our partner or friend perceives us.

After this, the commonest form of attack, the quality of criticism can become sinister. We are now not only reprimanded for an understandable human fault but we are taken to task about our very integrity. We are called liars, cheats, monsters, inhuman, accused of saying one thing and meaning another. We are assaulted verbally and our basic goodness is questioned. We are considered unreliable, unfaithful, dishonest, exploiters, and lacking in sensitivity. This process gradually undermines our value and significance and, if the attack is sustained, finally invalidates us. Everything which we took for granted in ourselves is slowly eradicated. We can reach the point when we no longer trust our judgment, our basic belief in ourselves, or our intentions. We can be driven in this way to madness as everything we ever believed in ourselves is destroyed.

Throughout the world this process is used as a form of torture, people are stripped of all their goodness and worth and then given the identity that an enemy wants them to have. This can happen in some relationships where we are invalidated to the point where we question everything basic about ourselves. If we accept the attack, we are filled with guilt and a sense of badness and our self-esteem takes a plunge. Our suffering is immense as we drown in the sea of personal doubt about our value. Such invalidation is frequently seen in marriages which go wrong, but is present in any close loving relationships where love is changed into suspicion and mistrust.

Total Rejection

The ultimate form of attack is complete rejection: we are no longer wanted. The culmination of pain in human relationships is the feeeling that one has been discarded; in other words that one has lost one's meaning to someone who previously held one in high esteem of love. This is the experience of the rejected spouse, parent and friend. If the rejection is mutual, the pain is still present but in muted form. If the rejection is unilateral, then an agonising state of suffering exists, as in the case of a spouse who still loves the departed partner or the parent who still loves the rejecting offspring. This was amply illustrated in the case of the father of the prodigal son.

Christ ultimately had to endure the pain of rejection not only by the society in which he lived but also by his own friends the apostles, who were too tired to pray with him and scattered out of fear. On the cross he went through the ultimate agony of separation; the excruciating pain of feeling abandoned by his own Father.

There is another form of pain, namely the feeling that we

have hurt someone we love. Guilt at having damaged our loved ones is a particularly penetrating hurt. Attack and counter-attack are the usual ways by which we deal with affronts to love, and if these exchanges continue and magnify the venom can gain the upper hand and the relationship be placed in jeopardy. Another response however is not to reply in kind but to withdraw, and this we do either because the pain is too severe or else as a way of punishing the aggressor. Either way, withdrawal or counter-attack, can ultimately destroy a loving relationship.

Beyond Forgiveness

The most immediate way out of any conflict is for the aggressor to apologise and seek forgiveness. This is the way in which we become reconciled daily to each other. If the wound has been particularly painful we need that extra quality of forgiveness we call mercy. The importance of forgiveness is illustrated in the gospels by the reply Christ gives to Peter: 'Then Peter went up to him and said, Lord, how often must I forgive my brother if he wrongs me? As often as seven times? Jesus answered, Not seven, I tell you, but seventy-seven times' (Matthew 18:21–2). Clearly the divine answer to offence is forgiveness, and in fact loving relationships are maintained by repeated mutual forgiveness. Yet we all know that although we can and do forgive seventy-seven times, sometimes the sheer repetition of the offence can and does become exasperating. We can take the hurt no more and the persistent misunderstanding becomes intolerable.

Far more serious is the fact that repetition of the same hurt suggests to us that our loving neighbour is not trying to overcome the problem. We begin to assume that he does not care, and our willingness to forgive is diluted by our resentment and frustration. There is a risk that our forgiveness may disappear unless we see a change in behaviour. Many marriages break down because one spouse loses hope that his/her partner will ever change. Nothing destroys love more effectively than the despair that is born of the belief that change will never come. Thus, at the heart of forgiveness, there must be both reparation and the seeds of change. Suffering becomes cruel when hope evaporates.

Beyond forgiveness there is the need to understand both oneself and one's attacker. Such understanding often belongs to the world of psychology, and this is one of the reasons why I believe that dynamic psychology is so essential to Christians. Forgiveness is essential but it is not enough. Unless we move from forgiveness to a change of behaviour we will not experience the deeper layers of loving. For me, the incarnation was a reconciliation between man and God, not only because God took upon himself the sins of man and made adequate reparation for our blindness, but even more important because his humanity was so complete that the pain of human deficiency could be converted into human integrity. In more traditional terms, the incarnation has opened the way from converting sin which is the negation of God, into love which is the reality and presence of God.

UNDERSTANDING OURSELVES

Ultimately the best way of understanding others is by understanding ourselves as fully as possible. When we do so, we can then go beyond the surface behaviour of others and try to understand their feelings.

There is always the danger that instead of appreciating the feelings of others we read into them our own hopes, expectations, standards, opinions, views and feelings; in other words, we project our own inner world on to others and then interpret it as theirs. If we clearly understand and recognise our feelings we can differentiate between our conscious and unconscious world and that of others.

If we are going to get beyond mutual recriminations in life, we must have a plan to deal with attacks. When we are attacked we must avoid as far as we can simply retaliating. We need to examine the nature of the criticism. Let us take the commonest form of criticism, that of selfishness. None of us will ever escape this attack. Are we really selfish? Do we put ourselves before others? Do we think about the needs of others? Are we sensitive to their particular sensitivities? Have we made it our job to find out what is going on in the inner world of the one we love? These are the questions we have to ask ourselves and then try to understand a little about ourselves.

As we have noted before, we all started life at the receiving end of attention. Our first experiences were of being given time, care, food and affection. Initially we responded blindly to parents, we were not aware of their inner world. We did not think or imagine that our parents had needs. We took their presence and nurturing for granted. Little by little we learned to recognise that parents and others existed, had requirements, and that we had a part to play in their life.

As adults we have constantly to examine our awareness of others. When we are accused of selfishness it is assumed that we put ourselves deliberately before others. Sometimes this happens because we are simply not aware of them. We may have been an only child, or lived with parents who were aloof and distant, with whom we rarely interacted. We may have been frightened, anxious, sickly children who used up all our energy just surviving with little left for noticing anybody else. In other words, our capacity to register the existence of others may be limited.

We may have the capacity to notice their presence and yet have little sense of what they need. We thus appear oblivious to the requirements of others. The husband is often accused of coming home, rarely asking how his wife is, sinking behind a paper, becoming glued to the television or withdrawing into a book, having no time for spouse or children. He appears markedly selfish and is told so. He in return pleads tiredness at the end of the day. Perhaps such a person grew up in an environment where he was not involved with parents or siblings. Doing things with others presupposes childhood involvement and where this was lacking the result is an adult of solitary habits.

Perhaps we are able to become involved, but insist on doing things our own way, being always right and tolerating no independent action from others. The consequences are easy to anticipate. We are told that we are selfish brutes hungry for power, intolerant and demanding. Perhaps we grew up in a home where we were totally dominated, organised and controlled. We know no other way of relating to others except by doing the same; or, more commonly, we have an anxious disposition and the only way we can cope with our anxiety is by controlling everyone else.

We may on the other hand interact with others without dominating them but at the same time remain oblivious to their feelings. With no idea when they are anxious, frightened, or need affection, support, encouragement, reassurance, we relate by expecting them to do their jobs and duties in a disciplined way as if they were soldiers acting automatically or governed by the pure dictates of reason and intellect. In such a relationship feelings do not exist, and those who do relate in his way are branded as insensitive and as people who never think of others. Yet only too often they will have grown up in a household where feelings are taboo and expressions of affection non-existent, or they may be men and women who find it exceedingly difficult to sense what others feel.

At this point someone will remark that all psychology does is to find a long list of excuses. In fact psychology is not there to excuse but to understand. When we are accused or when we accuse others of some crime, such as selfishness, we always assume that the accused has the insight and the freedom to act differently but deliberately refuses to do so. Often however neither insight nor freedom exists, at least initially. The point of psychology is to insert insight where none exists and to expand freedom of action to overcome existing limitations.

Thus when we are accused of selfishness the appropriate response of love is not to retaliate or make excuses but to search for the truth. The truth will be found either in our childhood or our make-up, or in a conjunction of both. We have to move from bland general accusations to specific issues and identify the problem in ourselves and in others. That is the first objective. Once we have identified the difficulty we have to begin to work at overcoming it. Traditionally the task of correction has been limited to criticism, to finding the fault, repeating the accusation and passing judgment, all of which is meant to induce guilt, a sense of badness and fear. But this merely adds insult to injury. Most people know when they are in the wrong and suffer enough from the consequences without additional burdens of guilt.

Our journey of guilt is through insight to change. We

have to help each other to understand behaviour in terms of deficiencies and limitations, not of badness. We do not encourage change when we impoverish the other's self-esteem. We ask for change out of love. When people change for the better everybody gains by becoming more loving. Once we have pinpointed each other's limitations, instead of criticising we can encourage and affirm. That is how we help the young to grow: we do our best to show them what is wrong and then reward all their efforts to change for the better; and the same pattern applies to adults. If we can begin to understand ourselves we can also interpret the conduct of others correctly. Once we have identified the problem we try to overcome it by helping each other, through encouragement and reward. This is the most productive move forward, which transforms accusation into loving understanding and encourages growth.

Mutual Insight

I have stressed the obligation of self-examination in depth, but in the presence of a loving relationship there is a development of mutual insight. A necessary part of loving is to help those we love to see and understand themselves more fully. We do this by helping them to clarify their confusion, giving them access to their unconscious, insight into their behaviour, and often simply by helping them to see themselves as others do. All this is very different from the vicious circle of mutual accusations.

When we move from mutual destruction to reciprocal growth, we recognise that in order to maintain a relationship of love we have to identify the problems that threaten to destroy it and overcome them. Our love is shown in the unceasing effort to recognise mutual problems and facilitate their defeat. This lifelong endeavour has its own pain but, like the pain of the woman in labour, it is most creative suffering.

THE CHRISTIAN EXPERIENCE

If we look at some of the older works of spiritual advice we discern an opinion that suffering is good for the soul, and indeed that the soul which has been made to suffer has been invested with particular grace. The point of all this suffering was that it should be joined to that of Christ, and so it was meant to be a welcome sign of God's favour. Thus, according to this tradition, pain should be welcomed and even sought. When it happened, it was to be embraced with enthusiasm and given up reluctantly. Suffering was a mark of spiritual distinction, and those who suffered any form of distress were summoned to do so with courage, patience and positive toleration. Suffering and death were linked, and death too was embraced as a release from this world which was after all a mere interval in the journey to eternity.

If death was to be welcomed, then inevitably spiritual counselling was directed towards the final ends of judgment, heaven and hell. This world was considered to be a passing phase, and suffering was there to direct our attention to the suffering of Christ, which we were invited to imitate. This approach to suffering suggested that God almost rejoiced in making humanity suffer. At times this God in his craving for human suffering approached the character of a sadistic God, and inevitably Christianity became masochistic, giving its blessing to a sado-masochistic alliance. The world rebelled decisively against such a God, and there are many people today who have left Christianity because of this approach.

Such an approach clearly forgot that our Lord was in no way a masochist who actually looked forward to his passion and death. He made it very clear that, if the cup could be removed, he would welcome the relief, and indeed his whole ministry showed compassion and a desire to relieve suffering. He healed the sick, relieved mental suffering, fed the hungry, and even raised the dead. Here was no proclivity to suffering for its own sake but, as with other aspects of his life, Christ joined suffering to love. There is the clue to the meaning of suffering.

Pain of Separation

At the heart of the incarnation is the separation of God the Father and God the Son. In order to accomplish his purpose Christ had to be physically separate from his Father, and an essential part of his life's suffering was the longing for reunion. The gospels tend to concentrate on Christ's suffering, death and resurrection, but in doing so we forget that at the heart of the Trinity is oneness and that an intrinsic part of love is union. Christ had to give up this union and live in a different context where he was misunderstood, reviled, rejected and ultimately killed. He did all this out of obedience to love. It was love that summoned him to take flesh and to surrender it back on the cross. So at the very centre of the incarnation is the suffering of separation and the longing for reunion.

Christ came to this earth in a state of poverty and, in accepting this form of childhood with its physical and social limitations, he embraced the suffering that is felt by all those who are lowly in status, role or power. He started the process of overcoming the world by climbing from its depths upwards. In doing so he encountered a great deal of suffering. His suffering started with the misunderstanding of his own family, who thought that his behaviour was mad. It extended into the circle of his friends the apostles, who were constantly misjudging his objectives. They wanted a Messiah who had power and authority in this world and would conquer. But he did nothing of the sort; instead he preached the kingdom of God which was based on love. Although they did not understand him they followed him and were like the crowd, amazed at everything he did.

In the meantime Christ continued to embrace suffering in his own life. Before starting his public ministry he withdrew into the desert, and there he fasted and prayed and was tempted. He was tempted with food, power and glory, and he repudiated them all. By his example he was teaching us that human emptiness has to be filled not by the rewards of this world, but by God, and he was rewarded by his Father's affirmation at his baptism and transfiguration. It was from his Father that he derived his meaning, his self-esteem and his love of self, and the discourses of St John's Gospel give full expression to this fullness which he derived from the Father. Thus Christ's lowly state, physical deprivation and acute disappointment at being misunderstood and rejected were the means through which he gave expression to the love of his Father. All this time he used his personal suffering to bring about conversion to his Father's ways. He did this by giving us the commandment to love our neighbour as ourselves and by pointing the way to its practical application in the sermon on the Mount and elsewhere. He overcame suffering wherever he met with it, and made it absolutely clear that suffering was not to be welcomed for its own sake but conquered through love. Wherever he saw suffering as a result of sin, the presence of evil, the devil, he used his love to conquer these messengers of destruction and in doing so demonstrated in individual lives that love will conquer. The ultimate conquest was that of death. Death paralysed life and brought love to a standstill. If love was to triumph, then death had to be defeated. In doing this Christ was expressing his love for everyone because his death had universal dimensions. Everybody was included in it.

He chose, and he repeats in the gospels that he chose freely, a particularly painful sort of death. To his social and spiritual alienation he now added the whole dimension of physical pain. In this way he made sure that there was no form of human suffering which he had not embraced and therefore transformed. Everything he touched, including suffering, was invaded by his love and thereby made purposeful and creative.

His death was ultimately to be followed by his resurrection, but before embracing it he felt its full horror and asked the Father to have it taken away. Abandoned by those he loved, cut off from his Father, he approached death with only love as his strength. He possessed himself totally in love and knew in the depth of himself that he could not deny the purpose of his life. He loved his Father and had to accomplish his Father's mission; he loved us and he had to show us that the ultimate suffering, which is death, can be conquered in love. Before actually dying he gave us himself as a gift of love, and so in the Eucharist we have a fusion of love and suffering by which suffering is overcome. His own cycle of suffering was concluded by his reunion with the Father. Christ's suffering is a model for our suffering. At its very centre is separation from the love of the Father, the incarnation and ultimate reunion. The ultimate criterion of love, however, is the maintenance of relationship. Christ maintained his relationship of love with his Father and in so doing met suffering face to face. He met it in the human condition, and his life, death

111

and resurrection constitute a cosmic event which has now transformed suffering. Before the incarnation suffering had taken a wrong turning. It was leading us away from our destiny with God and love. It was meaningless and pointless. When Christ embraced it, he brought about a crucial correction. Once again suffering became creative and part of the evolution of man towards God. Since Christ it now has a place as one of the ingredients of the completion of the universe. It cannot be escaped and it is not to be avoided. The world needs it for its progress, for its journey towards the omega point of meaning. The incarnation joined suffering to love, with the result that in our lives we need not be afraid of it.

Whether our suffering is peculiar to ourselves or whether it belongs to the society in which we live, it has to be handled ultimately with a loving response. It has to be resisted when it is destructive and embraced when it is creative. The criterion which helps us to distinguish between the two is whether it helps us to deepen our love of self, neighbour or God. When it does that, it is part of the positive force of creation; when it does not, it is inhuman and should be eliminated.

11

Aggression and the Image of God

The current debate about nuclear weapons is a reminder that violence expressed in war is likely to destroy all humanity and the interest in the nature of aggression has coincided with the awareness of this possibility. We are aware of many expressions of social aggression, including the destructiveness of football crowds, the pointlessness of vandalism and ultimately the expression of violence in our own lives and personal relations.

The question we have to ask is what are the origins of aggression. Is it innate, an intrinsic part of our nature from which we cannot escape, or is it a reaction to others and the environment, a force therefore that we can control personally or through the right measures in society? This is the familiar argument between nature and nurture. Is man born bad, one aspect of this badness being aggression; or is he born basically with a nature that is inclined to the good, with aggression being largely a positive expression and only occasionally destructive? These issues in turn lead us to ask questions about the nature of good and evil and about the nature of God. We are created in the image of God and, if this is the case, what we reflect expresses something fundamental about the nature of God. Is aggression part of God's nature? If so, is it something creative or destructive, and if something essentially creative, in what way has it been corrupted in man?

An examination of these questions will shed more light on the future of mankind. If man is basically aggressive in a destructive way, then mankind has no future because sooner or later it will use nuclear weapons and inevitably unleash a holocaust. If man is basically aggressive in a benign manner, then there is a chance that creativity will supplant ultimate destruction.

Let us look at what science has to say on the subject.

Innate Aggression

The pessimistic view of man is expressed in those theories that see destructive aggression as an innate part of human beings. There are two modern exponents of this view, Freud and Lorenz.

Freud is of course infinitely a greater contributor to the psychology of the human personality. His first formulation was that self-preservation and sexuality, or libido, were the two dominant forces in man. Later he came to the conclusion, based on a dual theoretical framework, that men and women possessed two instincts, namely life instinct (*eros*) and death instinct (*thanatos*), and he had this to say about the latter:

> Starting from the speculations on the beginning of life and from biological parallels, I drew the conclusion that, besides the instinct to preserve living substance, there must exist another contrary instinct, seeking to dissolve those units and to bring them back to their primaeval, inorganic state. That is to say that as well as *Eros* there was an instinct of death.

The death instinct is directed against oneself or others and it is essentially destructive, leading to disintegration.

On the surface this view of man believes that destruction is inevitable and is instinctive. In fact this is a simplification which does not do justice to Freudian theory. Freud recognised that man, driven by his instincts, the pleasure principle of *eros* and the aggressive principle of the death instinct, has to come to terms with reality, that which is allowed and permitted by parents and others. So behaviour is not a blind instinct. It is shaped by what is possible and permissible. The environment, in the form of parents, teachers and other figures of authority, acts as a controlling agent, and so our actual behaviour is the result on the one hand of what our instincts demand, and on the other of what is allowable; and so the pleasure and aggressive principles are controlled by

114

the reality principle and therefore man's behaviour is much more a calculated one than the result of blind forces.

Furthermore the *eros* or life preservation instinct develops into other characteristics of affection, love and tenderness and the development of these human traits is indicative of the wider possibilities in human beings beyond sheer destruction.

Thus the conclusion is that, although Freud's theory basically belongs to the category of innate destructive instincts, it is in fact markedly modifiable.

The next person to consider is Lorenz, who is basically a biologist and his deductions about man's aggression are inferred from observations in fish and birds. His conclusions are based on undiluted Darwinian evolution principles and he believes that man, like animals, is endowed with an aggressive instinct for self-preservation but which also exists in its own right, needs an outlet and, if one is not found, reaches explosive proportions.

In his book on *Aggression*, E. Fromm criticises Lorenz severely, showing that his conclusions are based on analogy from animals, are confused, that animals respond with aggression as a defence of their vital interests and that he does not distinguish a creative and a destructive element in human aggression.

I think it is possible to conclude from this section that a basic instinctive destructive drive has not been shown to exist unequivocally in mankind, although the aggressive potential for self-preservation, survival and creativity, and also for destructiveness, does exist.

Reactive Aggression
The alternative view is that the potential for both creative and destructive aggression in man is unleashed as a reaction to the environment, through personal and social forces. The psychological theory that fits in with this view is that of behaviourism. This theory has no basic view of how the human personality is made up. It is not concerned with instincts, unconscious motivation or moral forces. Its basic principles are very simple. What matters is the behaviour of people, what can be observed, recorded and measured, leading also to empirical, positive philosophy. What actually

motivates behaviour are rewards and punishments. Whatever rewards facilitates a pattern of behaviour which is then repeated and whatever punishes inhibits behaviour which is curtailed. Rewards in technical jargon reinforce behaviour and, in the case of aggression, which is taken for granted, whatever makes aggression pay is repeated and maximised.

A particular expression of behaviourism in relation to aggression is the theory of frustration. Whenever an ongoing, goal-directed activity is frustrated or a desire or wish is denied, then aggression follows. An example of the first is being caught in a traffic jam and of the second is the reaction when we are told we cannot have something we want. It is true that in both circumstances anger can be experienced but it is not inevitable and sometimes frustration becomes an opportunity for creativity expressed in the saying that 'necessity is the mother of invention'. But human experience teaches us that frustration is not only an inevitable source of aggression but it is a human reaction that can be trained. A child reacts to frustration with a greater tendency to aggression than an adult who has been gradually trained to cope with such an experience.

Thus so far we can see that the psychological interpretations of aggression range from a narrow reading of psychoanalytic instinctive drives to simple responses to the environment which can be frustrating. The evidence demonstrates beyond any doubt that aggressive responses exist but the arguments continue whether such aggression is blind and unmodifiable or open to personal and social forces which can alter it. Eric Fromm, who has evaluated the available evidence in detail, comes to the conclusion that there is nothing inevitable about it but that biological tendencies do exist which respond to the environment. The familiar argument between nature and nurture, between heredity and environment, is recast in terms of an interaction between the two.

Biological Drive

As far as human beings are concerned the biological basis of aggression is still largely not understood, but three things are known. First there are parts of the brain which are intimately

116

connected with aggression. Secondly, in animal studies the male hormone testosterone, which is present in much larger quantities in the male than the female, is linked with aggressive behaviour. Thirdly, the Y chromosome which is responsible for maleness is also linked with aggression because, in a few individuals who have a double YY chromosome, there is a tendency for them to be more aggressive. Hence aggressiveness is linked much more with the male than the female and, although both sexes are capable of showing aggressive behaviour, the evidence on the whole implicates the male as being the more aggressive of the two.

Human Aggression

What I have written so far suggests that human aggression, which undoubtedly exists, is not a simple evolution of animal behaviour but has specific human characteristics. What are these special human features? Fromm refers to human aggression as being an expression of our very humanity. Although we have links with animals, men and women have the capacity for imagination, creativity, foresight, planning, controlling and, above all, relating to others in a personal way in which love and hate exist. Thus their aggression is both destructive or malignant, and benign or creative. If we are to understand human aggression it is important to examine these two varieties.

Benign Aggression

First, there is defensive aggression. When our vital interests are threatened, particularly our life, we can either fly or fight. Often we fly, but sometimes we have no choice but to fight. Equally we may also fight for some special cause, opinion or value that is important to us. In this response human beings use aggression in a positive way to protect life, property or some specific value.

One specific value which is totally human is the protection of freedom. We protect our personal freedom, that of our society and of our country, with a vehemence that is second to none. Aggression in the interest of freedom takes many forms and sometimes freedom is fought for when the odds are heavily in favour of the oppressor. Men and women will sacrifice their life on its behalf, and in the post-war period we have seen freedom fighters all over the world battling for their independence.

The fight for freedom and independence has also expanded enormously in the relationship between persons. Young people fight their parents, wives are asserting their independence from men, women are fighting for their rights, the laity in the Church have rebelled against authoritarianism. There is a widespread use of aggression, both physical and verbal, for freedom and one's own rights.

Another feature, which is even more psychological, is one's self-esteem. All of us strive to have a positive image of our body, mind and feelings. The sum total of these positive experiences gives us the feeling of being of value, worthwhile and lovable. When our self-esteem is attacked we can react violently because the very basis of our being is being undermined. We shall return to this theme again; but we must distinguish between self-esteem and egoism or self-centredness. In the case of the latter we are protecting false images of ourselves; in the former instance we are protecting something essential to the very core of our being.

Intimately related to self-esteem is the question of trust. If we do not trust another person physically, emotionally or socially, we are on our guard. A special feature of human defensive aggression as opposed to the animal variety is that animals respond very much to a here-and-now threat to survival whereas man has the capacity to visualise the future. This is a profoundly important difference because as human beings we take precautions against both real and imaginary dangers. A good deal of aggressive behaviour is linked with anticipated threat which in turn is based on the fact that we do not trust others. We protect ourselves with security systems because we do not trust the burglar-to-be. In America they arm themselves with real guns for protection. The world is now locked in building up nuclear forces, which are called defensive, because we do not trust each other's motives.

We can also be aggressive because we obey legitimate authority. Soldiers obey commands. This type of aggression is necessary to defend our countries but it is also potentially dangerous. Blind obedience can be manipulated and indeed the capacity to manipulate public opinion to see another country as dangerous, wicked or evil and to attack it is one of the real dangers of human society.

Destructive Aggression

When we look at the destructive type of aggression we move to the other end of the continuum of all these characteristics.

Starting with defence, we proceed to the point when we are not content with defending ourselves but actually wish to destroy the person who attacks us. The motivation to do this may be fear, the need to ensure that the attacker is eliminated and is no longer a threat to us. Fear plays a vital role in killing and destroying an enemy, humiliating our opponents, making sure that those we vanquish will not rise again to be a threat to us. Our fear and insecurity prompt us to go beyond defence in the direction of actually eliminating whatever threatens us.

This fear is reinforced by the feeling of vengeance. When we get hurt in any way one of the human reactions, not noticeable in animals, is to avenge ourselves on anyone who hurts or threatens us. It is a reaction which is clearly distinguishable from defending ourselves. Revenge occurs after the danger to us is over and expresses a deep desire to hurt back. This desire can be cruel to the extreme and some of the worst features of human cruelty result from acts of revenge. Revenge of course leaves a deep sense of injustice and hatred in those so treated and a vicious circle of hatred and revenge can be established which can last for centuries, as we see in Ireland, the fight between Jews and Arabs, Greeks and Turks and many other peoples. Unfortunately revenge can play a part in religious aggression and some of the worst bloodshed in human history occurs on religious grounds.

Closely associated with revenge are the mysterious human characteristics of sadism and masochism, in which we actually derive pleasure from inflicting pain on another person or from receiving pain. The roots of sadism and masochism are manifold and complex and they are intensely destructive. When the infliction or reception of pain is combined with sex, then we have the more classical meanings of sadism and masochism.

Most of the really malignant forms of aggression are peculiar to human beings and not present in animals, which use aggression for obvious reasons such as defence, obtaining food, protecting their territory and safeguarding the sexual mate, and then often aggression is limited to achieving the objective without inflicting undue damage to the aggressor except when the prey has to be killed for food.

There is something specific about human beings which make them subject to extreme behaviour. Essentially human beings need others to relate to and to love. If man finds himself unable to relate, he can do a number of things. He can make contact with bodies without relation, which is the essence of promiscuity with its destructiveness. If he cannot relate freely, he coerces through fear, domination, control or tyranny. If he cannot relate in any of these ways, he can ultimately destroy others by killing them so that their presence does not taunt or haunt him or he can destroy himself by committing suicide. More commonly he emotionally eliminates those with whom he is unable to relate by pretending they do not matter to him or that he loves aloneness. Another way of coping with aloneness is through oblivion, either through alcohol, drugs or more commonly by incessant pseudo-mutuality, in endless parties where he is constantly in the presence of others but does not relate to anyone, and at times of difficulty or need no one is available to help. All these forms of aggression are persistently malignant forms of overcoming aloneness.

Finally when we establish closeness, this is done through the bonds of affection and love. When we love we go some way to making ourselves totally available to another human being. If we love authentically we do not wish to possess them as objects but respect them as persons and pay due regard to their freedom, independence, rights and needs. The opposite destructive characteristics are oppression, demanding submission and blind obedience, ignoring their rights or needs; and really much malignant aggression is perpetrated in unloving personal relationships where we ignore or tyrannise those we are supposed to love. Indeed if our loved one is treated as an object, we are terrified of losing them and direct wanton aggression to anyone who threatens our possession. But ultimately, woe to the person who repudiates our love. If our love is rejected we suffer an immense hurt and occasionally our anger is so immense that we attack physically and even kill. Much violence is perpetrated within the family which stems ultimately from this rejection.

The Image of God in Man
Where does all this leave us with our pursuit of the image of God in man? Clearly if we believe that man's basic nature is bad, wicked or evil, then destructive aggression is seen as part of this make-up and humanity is doomed to evil. Some fundamental Christian groups approach man with this rooted conviction of his badness. The trouble with this view is that in this case, if man reflects the image of God, then God in some way must have this destructive element of aggression as part of his natutre. Is this the case? In order to understand the relationship between aggression and God we must look at revelation and at the life of Jesus Christ.

Clearly revelation discloses that God could be and was frequently angry with man. Psalm 90 first describes how man is burned by God's anger and terrified by his fury. Later on the psalm says:

Who yet has felt the full force of your fury
or learnt to fear the violence of your rage? (Psalm 90:11)

The Old Testament repeatedly describes God's anger and the punishments he meted out to his errant people. All this anger was for their good and forgiveness was equally a constant theme.

In the New Testament anger and aggressive behaviour are clearly recognised in men and women, but the teaching is absolutely constant; anger has to be overcome by love, aggression by forgiveness, attack by offering the other cheek. There is an increasing proclamation that destructive aggression is not part of God's image in man. The following passage from Luke makes us tremble with the sheer wonder of the message:

But I say this to you who are listening: love your enemies, do good to those who hate you; bless those who curse you, pray for those who treat you badly. To the man who slaps you on one cheek, present the other cheek too; to the man who takes your cloak from you, do not refuse your tunic. Give to everyone who asks you, and do not ask for your property back from the man who robs you. Treat others as you would like them to treat you. If you love those who love you, what thanks can you expect? Even sinners love those who love them. And if you do good to those who do good to you, what thanks can you expect? For even sinners do that much. And if you lend to those from whom you hope to receive, what thanks can you expect? Even sinners lend to sinners to get back the same amount. Instead, love your enemies and do good, and lend without any hope of return. You will have a great reward, and you will be sons of the Most High, for he himself is kind to the ungrateful and the wicked. (Luke 6:27–35)

The implications of this passage are momentous and really have a direct bearing on war. If this teaching of Christ was implemented fully, then we would let aggressors have their way in the conviction that in the long run they will be converted by our love. The rational arguments against such behaviour are legion. It is said that, if we give in to aggression, we simply encourage it. If we don't protect ourselves, we lose our freedom and we are destroyed. Basically Christ is saying that such loss is a way of finding life for he who loses his life finds it. There is no doubt that the cost of peace in Christian terms is enormous. On the other hand, with nuclear weapons, what is the cost of war?

As far as Christ is concerned, his life did show the whole range of benign aggression. He protected himself from the Jews by fleeing from them until he was ready to give up his life. He was not afraid to protect himself from unnecessary aggression by the Jews. In the ordinary exchanges with them, he argued fiercely and aggressively for his point of view and did not mince his words in favour of the truth. He carried his aggression to action when he overturned the tables of the moneylenders in the Temple. He rebuked the Devil frequently, and also his own apostles, not least Peter. What is more, he healed the ravages of aggression on the body and mind and pacified the aggression of nature by calming the waves and the winds.

In the end he did precisely what he preached. He suffered verbal and physical violence and gave his life for us. Part of the eternal integrity of Christ is the fact that what he said and did coincided and in one stroke reconciled all man's tensions within himself. But of destructive aggression, we see not a single trace. Revenge, hate, retaliation, destructiveness, none of these exists in his life. So the conclusion that we must draw on the basis of revelation and the life of Jesus Christ is that aggression, in a creative, benign form, is indeed to be found in the life of God and, in so far as man is created in his image, man too expresses it. We find no trace of destructive aggression in the life of God, the Father, Son or Spirit.

As far as Christianity is concerned, we need to learn important lessons. Traditional piety has led us to believe that any expression of aggression is inconsistent with Christian life. We have had, in the past, images of sanctity which have been nauseatingly inhuman and, in my view, have contributed to the indifference shown to religion as human beings have found that it did not correspond to authentic experience. This has been increasingly true in the last hundred years with the rise of Freudian psychology which has placed so much importance on aggression. The benign form of aggression is an essential part of being human.

But Christianity is not a faith that simply authenticates human integrity. It does more than that; it invites us to participate in the very essence of being divine. In other words, in the teachings of Christ we find a way of life that not only removes destructive aggression, not only approves benign aggression, but sets the path to perfection, to the fullness of the divine image.

Here we move from aggression to love and we are asked to forsake even benign aggression for the sake of love.

Christ himself expressed benign aggression but ultimately cooperated with the Father, converting his humanity to its full divine potential.

We are asked to do no less. The price of converting

aggression to love is a high one and each and everyone of us has to pursue it in our Christian life. There are no short cuts and the way forward is slow and painful but this conversion is an essential part of being Christian. In the next chapter, we shall examine how we can move in that direction.

12

Aggression and Love

In this chapter we shall examine the relationship between aggression and love. As Christians we are invited to love our neighbour as ourselves and one of the principal distractions in effecting this is aggression, expressed as anger in relationship to oneself and others.

Aggression and Self
We have seen that anger as an expression of aggression is a human potential which everyone possesses to a variable degree. It can be expressed verbally or physically although in our society the shift from one to another is a movement from permissible benign aggression to the unacceptable malignant form. We recognise that anger has a legitimate part in our life and Christ certainly used it, but we are often unsure what are the permitted areas of benign aggression.

Following our biological roots, it is clear that we have a right to protect our life and, psychologically, our self-esteem. We are entitled to defend ourselves from physical and verbal assault. The extreme form of attack on our life can be an occasional rare event or something quite common, depending on where we live, but the bruising of our image of ourselves is a much more frequent phenomenon. Both those close to us and our enemies can hurt us by questioning our honesty, integrity, justice, values and opinions. They can call us hypocrites by trying to show the disparity between our good intentions and our deeds. They seek to denigrate our achievements and, in the name of humility, reduce our worth. This persistent devaluation of ourselves is a very good reason for getting angry. We are obliged to defend not only our life, but its significance, and anyone who threatens either should not be surprised if we rush to our own defence.

Those who attack us can and do hurt us and when we get hurt a natural response is to get angry. Often we get hurt not by our enemies, from whom we expect little else, but by those who claim to love us. In this case it is important to declare our feelings of hurt otherwise they will never know what impact they have on us; otherwise we cannot change things. One of the real hurts we experience in life is through the expectation that those who love us can read us accurately and not say or do things that upset us. We live with the conviction that they will know us as intimately as our parents and behave accordingly, without us having to tell them anything about our inner world. Often they fail in this perspicacity and we feel badly let down. Anger is a signal of our real needs and it is one way of educating those who love us in the contents of our inner world. Of course we have to move beyond anger and explain in detail but sometimes we cannot do this because we do not understand ourselves fully and we can only react through anger.

Beyond hurt and attack, there exists the simple necessity of asserting one's existence. From the moment we are born until we die we need to be heard, recognised, appreciated and responded to. When we are very young we show this need by crying, and tears of frustrated anger can accompany us throughout life. Whenever we find ourselves in danger of being ignored or dismissed, we need to assert our existence and, although there are many ways of doing this, anger certainly produces results. In the course of a day we can be reduced to a sense of helpless impotence unless we assert our right to be.

Those who are wounded in the course of their childhood in their self-esteem, or who felt ignored, may over-react later on in life and either defend or assert themselves with a vehemence that astonishes others. In fact these people are fighting for their very existence and their exaggerated stance is often a reflection of their desperation. Indeed it is often from the pool of these desperate men and women that aggression changes from verbal to physical. They often feel that their words will carry no conviction and they want to underline their message with a degree of violence which unfortunately only estranges them further from those they are trying to influence.

Physical violence is of course not only a reaction to desperation, it can be something that has been seen and learned at home, so that violence is not necessarily always an expression of frustration.

Anger and Guilt

We know from ordinary experience that giving vent to our anger is not a simple matter. One of the painful consequences is that we feel guilty when we get angry with others, particularly those we love. In Christian thought guilt has been related so often to the violation of rules or linked simply with our supposed innate badness that we pay little attention to the origins of guilt feelings. These spring from the feelings of badness, remorse and distress that we experience when we are angry with the most important person in our life, namely our parents. Anger separates us from them, hurts them and temporarily makes us feel extremely uncomfortable. Yet, if we are to separate and assert our independence, we need to get angry and so the link between anger and guilt is established. This link extends to all those who are close to us, our spouses, children and friends, and we find it particularly difficult to express anger in these circumstances. On the other hand, as we have already seen, it is those who are close to us who are likely to hurt us and provoke our aggression, so that the family is often the classic place where tensions are experienced.

If we suppress our anger by a conscious and deliberate action or it has become repressed over the years, that is to say rendered unconscious, then a number of things can happen. If we sit on our anger and simply suppress it, then it bubbles inside us and one day, when we can no longer control ourselves, when we are tired, or irritable, we actively explode. Then all hell is let loose and all the accumulated resentment spills over and the consequent guilt feelings can overwhelm us. In fact we can become secondarily angry for having become so guilty. If we do not explode but go on entertaining our suppressed anger, we can become depressed or act out our resentment in other ways by being uncooperative and generally difficult.

In the end we have to recognise that being angry often hurts us and the person we love. We try to avoid it and effect the desired change in other ways but when this does not succeed anger needs to come out.

Anger and Destruction

Sometimes we hold our anger back because we are afraid that if we unleash it we shall set in action a trail of destruction. We can be terrified of our aggression and entertain in our phantasy horrible images of what we will do to others if we had the chance. All of us have our favourite dialogue in which we silence our foe, humiliate them to extinction and we may even indulge in imagining the variety of ways in which we would kill our mother-in-law or our boss.

We know only too well that in practice we will do nothing of the sort and that we are in fact meek and mild, that our roar turns into a squeak. Sometimes, however, we have not got our phantasies under control. They are truly unconscious and threaten us with a sense that we will be omnipotently and disastrously destructive. These fears are the remnants of childhood phantasies when our aggression could overwhelm us and we had no effective means of handling it. Over the years we can be tortured by the feeling that if we let go, then the consequences might be disastrous.

Occasionally a person who is afraid of his/her anger finds in practice that they can be truly lethal and annihilate their opponents. Such destructive display frightens them and they return to repressed controlled behaviour. Often however our phantasies picture an infinitely more damaging possibility than reality. When we let out our anger we find that nothing too terrible happens and our worst fears are not realised.

Even those who realise that they can be extremely angry can learn through help to moderate their outbursts, particularly when their complaints have been recognised and met. Sometimes the anger we experience towards others remains unexpressed and we turn it towards ourselves. If we feel impotent to influence others, we can become convinced that our cause is hopeless and turn the full might of our anger against ourselves. This is one reason for suicide. Often however we begin to feel bad when we are angry and blame ourselves for our behaviour. Then we get into a psychological tangle. When we were young we were conditioned to feel bad when we were angry, and we continue to feel bad when we are angry as adults. Instead of recognising the damage others do to us and feeling righteous about being angry, we respond by feeling bad and guilty. The result is a nightmare. We feel hurt when others attack us but instead of responding back, we increase our feelings of being bad and guilty if we try to defend ourselves. Such people cannot extricate themselves from this psychological mess and need to be rescued if they are not ultimately to destroy themselves through the sheer agony of despair.

Expression of Anger

While a few find expressing anger easy, the vast majority of people find it difficult to impossible. One way of dealing with frustrated anger is to displace it. The frustrated employee, who cannot get angry with his boss, comes home and takes it out on his wife and children. If he finds it difficult to get cross with his family, he discharges his fury on the cat or some other inanimate object. The person who is nice to everyone except his wife and children is a familiar figure of complaint in marriage.

The moral of all this is that we need to educate our children to be angry and to learn how to handle their anger so that they grow up feeling they can be angry when necessary. The freedom to be angry is the key to control. Traditionally we were taught to suppress our anger but this is not the answer to human aggression. In so far as it takes a benign form, we need to have the freedom to express it or not. Only when we have this freedom can we go beyond and actually withold our anger. When we feel emotionally able to be angry when necessary, then we have reached the really loving position of feeling that sometimes though anger is justified, it is not the most persuasive weapon to change another's behaviour. Withholding our anger out of love in circumstances where we could have expressed it if necessary is a very different matter from suppressing our anger out of fear, guilt or the inability to express it. In this way we acquire the ability to go beyond anger to authentic love.

Some people in counselling circles, having misread Freud, believe that the articulation of anger is a compulsive necessity because anger is seen as an innate hydraulic force which must be evacuated at regular intervals. We have seen that this deterministic biological blind force interpretation of aggression is not true. Man has the capacity to be angry in certain circumstances of defence, hurt and assertiveness and he needs to have the freedom to do so but he does not need to exercise it if other means can be equally effective.

Thus the ultimate goal of anger is to learn how to use it when it matters. We do not arrive at this point easily. Those who cannot express it at all have to learn to do so and in the process of learning will either exaggerate or underplay their feelings, but gradually they will find a happy medium. Those who are constantly angry can learn that anger can become a way of life and they need to unlearn their peculiar style of relating. They may find that when their needs and aspirations have been recognised they are no longer angry.

Some people are caught in the trap of never feeling secure and their self-esteem depends on the diminution of others. Couples can play this game – when one is up the other is down – and so anger is exchanged in a constant battle of retaliation. When one is angry the other responds with anger because they cannot exchange anything else. Anger can become ultimately a weapon of impotence and frustration, but that is not its purpose. The purpose of anger is to defend our integrity and to inform others when we are hurt.

Aggression Towards Oneself

This leads me to the issue of how we respond to anger against us. As Christians we are invited to love our neighbour as ourselves, and indeed to love our enemies. I find in this commandment the ultimate link between anger and love and I want to consider this.

It is clear that the way we receive the anger of others will be determined by our image of ourselves and by our sensitivity. If we react to anger as a form of criticism, rebuke and a declaration of our badness, then we simply take up a defensive position. We retaliate, defend ourselves and counter-attack, and the more vulnerable we are the greater is the likelihood that we will respond negatively. Whether we can love our friendly critics, whether we can decode the message of hurt from others, whether we can ultimately love our enemies depends on our self esteem or the love of ourselves.

As described previously, love of self means that, first of all, we feel in possession of ourselves, which in turn means that we are in touch with our bodies, minds and feelings and truly feel that we own them. This in turn means that we have separated from our parents and do not feel that we belong to them, that we do not live by their kind permission. It means we do not need the approval of figures of authority. Ultimately we need to feel that we have a right to exist and are not merely tolerated. If we do not possess ourselves, then the aggression of others threatens our very existence. We feel that, if we are not careful, they will destroy the tentative hold we have over ourselves and so we fight fiercely for survival. Our love for the underdog is a constant refrain in our society for in a sense we were all underdogs when we were small and the threat of being annihilated remains. The fierce resistance put up by those whose survival is threatened most easily is one way we can all respond to aggression if our own tenure of ourselves is delicate. Beyond possessing ourselves, we need to feel that what we own is good, sound, reliable and trust-worthy. If we feel that, the most persistent onslaught against us will not elicit a counter-offensive because we are not threat-ened. We know that we are sound, reliable, good, and the gates of hell cannot prevail against it. So our self-esteem blunts the assaults of others and we are free to see beyond their anger, to attend to their needs because we do not have to defend ourselves. The person who feels good can love his enemies because he has nothing to fear from them. Ulti-mately, even if we are taken over, we retain our goodness under tyranny. Even if we are killed, our goodness is not destroyed. The aggression of the other has no power over us because we cannot be intimidated. For me this represents most fully the personality of Christ. He possessed himself fully and he felt totally good about himself and in this way he could love his enemies because their aggression could not alter his identity. That is what we are striving for too. This is the goal of Christian life in personal terms. But we know that we are often some distance from this objective, so what is the reality we have to pursue. Even here Christ shows the way. The model is to beware the destruction of others and yet to approach everyone with the unceasing and renewed hope that we can trust them and love can ensue.

John tells us:

> During his stay in Jerusalem for the Passover many believed in his name when they saw the signs that he gave; but Jesus knew them all and did not trust himself to them; he never needed evidence about any man; he could tell what a man had in him. (John 2:23–5)

Here and in other passages we see Christ perpetually on the alert, aware of human limitations and therefore on his guard but at the same time never despairing. He encouraged constant forgiveness and renewed effort. 'If your brother does something wrong, reprove him and if he is sorry, forgive him. And if he wrongs you seven times a day and seven times comes back to you and says, I am sorry, you must forgive him' (Luke 17:3–4). For me this and other passages suggest that one definition of love is staying in relationship however hard this may be. Remaining in relationship means that, in the end, beyond hurt and aggression, there will emerge mutual recognition, appreciation, affection and love. But staying in relationship can also become a form of attenuated boredom and indifference. Clearly staying in relationship which aims at loving your partner or friend reconciles continuing presence with unfolding concern.

In particular I want to draw attention to the person who is persistently aggressive towards us. We tend to think that such behaviour is tiresome and indeed it is. When our spouse, dear friend, relative, or employer attacks us continuously, we wonder why we should stay and continue to suffer the onslaught. Very often the person who attacks us unremittingly both loves us and is desperately in need of our attention. If he or she did not love us, they would simply give up. But their constant attacks suggest a deep sense of unhappiness which they are waiting for us to recognise and remedy. It is surprising how the fury of another abates when we respond accurately to their inner needs.

Often the apparently strong and aggressive person is very insecure and fragile underneath and, unless we see this, we can go on interpreting their behaviour as a massive demonstration of strength when it is a shrieking scream of helplessness. We are amazed to find the apparently strong man or woman ending up becoming unconscious with drink or taking an overdose.

Behind the apparent combination of adult dominance and aggressivity, there often lies a sensitive, insecure, frightened and fragile child screaming to be rescued. We see this, I think, in Peter's behaviour in the gospels. He was always making grand shows of confidence and yet showing his fear when he tried to walk on the water and his panic when he betrayed Christ three times. But Christ, who had to rebuke him often, remained in relationship with him and after Pentecost the frightened child became the head of the Church and led it successfully.

Beyond Forgiveness

I have referred to Christ's teaching of loving our neighbour and constant forgiveness. Forgiveness is the opposite of malignant aggression, which takes the form of revenge. When aggression is directed against us, we can become hurt. When aggression is directed towards our family, we want to hit back and hurt the aggressor. When we see the innocent attacked, women raped, cruelty inflicted, children molested, the young and the old damaged, the core of our being cries for revenge, and yet we are invited to forgive as Christ did on the cross. Certainly forgiveness is the opposite side of the coin from hurt and damage, and indeed we do forgive. Christ stresses that we must not only forgive those we love but also the stranger and the unknown. Nevertheless it is those who are close to us that we forgive most often.

The point I want to make here is that forgiveness is not enough. We need to go beyond forgiveness and do as Christ did, who knew what was in man. We must try to understand what lies behind the act of aggression. One set of reasons is that the aggressor himself is hurt, insecure, vulnerable, bored, tired, depressed, confused, under stress and is seeking help through aggression. If that is the case, it is not good enough to forgive, we have to do something about remedying the cause of his aggression.

Even more important, the cause may be ourselves. There is nothing more hypocritical in Christian life than to forgive the aggressor with magnanimity when in actual fact we are responsible for his aggression. The woman who forgives her husband for having an affair when she denies him love and affection is no saint. The parent who forgives the errant child who is not allowed their independence and is constantly devalued and undermined is no saint. The friend who forgives while driving their companion to distraction is no saint.

The hardest thing to do is in effect to look at our own contribution to the frustrating aggression of those close to us. I would go further and say that whenever we have cause to forgive anybody, we should at the same time examine our own behaviour to see what provocation we have offered which contributes to the offence. Sometimes we do not recognise our own simmering anger which expresses itself indirectly by being difficult, to which the other responds by aggression.

So beyond forgiveness we need to understand the cause of the offence and see to what extent we or social conditions provoke this behaviour or whether we are responding accurately and sensitively to the needs of others. What they need from us is encouragement and help when they try to change their behaviour. Above all they need plenty of appreciation and affirmation. The best way to diminish the aggression of others is to attend to their needs, to encourage their efforts to change and to pat them on the back when they have achieved the smallest progress. Often we do not do this. When people annoy us, we want them to change. When they do try to change, we do not help them in the process because we feel they should not be like this or that from the start. When they are struggling to change to meet us, all we want is for them to hurry up and alter without caring too much how they achieve it. The cost of change is enormous. We forget that Christ had to die to fill the world with energy to change in the direction of love. We ignore those who are trying to meet us at our peril. Either they give up in despair and cease to try or they succeed without us and find in the end they do not need us. The journey of conversion from aggression to love needs the intermediate stations of our love, understanding, support and appreciation. Then forgiveness is complete.

13

The Meaning of Anxiety

What is Anxiety

Let us start by asking the question, what is anxiety? It is a state which affects both the mind and the body. In a moment I shall describe the physical characteristics of anxiety but everyone has experienced a funny feeling in the pit of the stomach before examinations or driving tests, being summoned by authority or before an operation. Anxiety is a red light that flickers on and off in our lives at frequent intervals, depending on how anxious we are and what is happening in our life.

There is a very old argument in science as to whether it is the anxiety of the mind that switches on the symptoms in the body or the symptoms in the body which give rise to the sensations in the mind. It does not matter, both occur.

How does anxiety manifest itself? The earliest mental manifestation is a sense of discomfort, a cringing feeling; for example, what some people feel at the sight of blood. Incidentally, anxiety does not respect size or gender. The following is a true story. I went up to university with a friend who had been at the same school and who was a burly great rugby player, who later played for the university. One day we were watching an experiment on a rabbit and, behold, one moment my friend was standing upright and the next he was on the floor flat out, looking like death itself.

However, most people get progressive warnings that their discomfort is rising and next it becomes fear. Fear is the commonest manifestation of anxiety. We are afraid of many things, of heights, of open spaces, closed places, pain, anger; indeed there is no human situation or activity that some people are not afraid of. Often we keep our fears to ourselves because we are ashamed to betray our secret. What is surprising is that when we start talking about our fears, other people are liberated to talk about theirs.

During the period of religion in which I grew up there was a strong notion that God watched and knew our inner secrets from which we could not escape punishment. (So often it was hinted that these inner secrets, which were also our fears, were sexual in nature). That was part of the vertical sense of God and religion in which one was locked in a personal relationship with God and there was no escape from the eternally vigilant eye of the Father who saw and punished. Today the self-help, counselling and community awareness is teaching us that sharing our inner world with others is a process of liberation leading to growth and maturity. So that sharing our fears helps us to discover that many others have fears too and we break from our isolation.

The next step from fear is an escalation into panic. This is aproaching the point where our mental and physical powers begin to disintegrate. In a minor way at the beginning of panic we are so anxious that we don't hear what is being said to us. Very anxious people sometimes complain that they have a poor memory. This is often due to the fact that they are too anxious to register what is being delivered to them. (Just in case you are alarmed – or perhaps relieved – there are other causes of poor memory!) But as the panic escalates, all control is lost. During war soldiers who are panicking have been known to run towards the enemy as their sense of direction and purpose has been lost. In outbreaks of danger, such as fire or in crowded situations, panic may ensue as people lose control of themselves.

Finally the panicking person finishes in a heap of terror totally incapable of functioning and I presume the last few seconds before serious accidents render the victims incapable in this way. But I think it is worth remembering that people can get into this state of panic about social and moral issues and it is not just physical events that can terrify us.

I have just described the mental manifestations of anxiety but that is not the whole story. There are physical ones as well. The automonic system controls such parts of our body as our heart, respiration, gastrointestinal system, sweating, etc. Under conditions of anxiety, all these organs become hyperactive and so we get vasodilatation and blushing, sweating, breathlessness, palpitations and – at its extreme – diarrhoea. Perhaps the most frequent manifestation is that we want to empty our bladder frequently under conditions of stress. All these symptoms are familiar to the sufferers and to doctors. It is easy, for example, to detect that one is meeting an anxious person by the sweating palm of the handshake or the blushing manifestation over some awkward subject.

All these physical manifestations are usually temporary at the height of a crisis but some people become chronically saddled with the symptoms and then what is a normal manifestation of anxiety becomes an illness. Anxiety neurosis is measured by the intensity and duration of symptoms.

Purpose of Anxiety

So what is the purpose of all these features of anxiety? Why should we become anxious? After all, the manifestations mentioned are all unpleasant. There is however a point to it all. In the Darwinian theory of evolution what is postulated is the survival of the fittest. In other words, we have to adapt to our environment successfully if we are going to survive. Anxiety is part of a triad of pain and depression which together combine to help us survive.

Anxiety is something we share with animals and it is essential for their survival. It is the means of alerting us to danger. An animal in the wild is constantly open to the risk of attack and its survival depends on its ability to sense danger and to do one of two things; either fight or flee. We human beings have also at times to fight or to flee. We have to protect our nation at times of war. We have to protect our homes from intruders, but most of our protection is no longer against physical dangers but against social and psychological risks. Today the world is faced with famine, nuclear war, extinction of its resources, pollution, economic exploitation, social prejudice and unemployment. Anxiety alerts us to injustice, to social danger and to extinction from man-made destruction.

In the spiritual field, anxiety makes us aware of evil and sin and the answer which is God. I shall return to this in a moment but what I am trying to present is the evolution of anxiety from a response to physical danger to that of a social, psychological and spiritual dimension. Man is now conditioned to be aware of human catastrophe which in turn has a divine remedy of love.

I have mentioned two other warning signals and they need a moment spent on them. Depression is the response to loss. Depression and anxiety often go together and certainly depression is a feature which we also share with animals. Depression is a time of sorrow, distress, reduction of activity and sadness over the loss of a person, thing or relationship. It is the loss of relationship, attachment or bonding which is crucial and conjoins the protection of the young and the partner in the animal world and that of the family in humans. The presence of mate and children are essential features of survival and the loss of either is a crucial deprivation. Finally pain is also a warning to protect the body and the mind from the deleterious effects of disease and acts as a precaution to take steps.

The three features of anxiety, depression and pain are at the biological level the means of human survival. But men and women have to go beyond death. They have become aware of immortality, of a dimension which takes them beyond life and death to a vision of eternity. The Greeks had already discovered the notion of immortality and the Christian revelation spells out that death is not the end.

This leads me to the relationship between anxiety and salvation. Most of us grew up with a very restricted view of salvation, focussed on the state of our immortal soul at the time of death. Hence the emphasis on last-minute conversion or confession. This was an era which was obsessed with the details of mortal and venial sin and much anxiety was expanded by Roman Catholics as to whether they were in one state or another. Frequent confession was the order of the day and much anxiety was aroused by the fear of being out of favour with God as prescribed by the catechism. Today we realise that, although sin exists, its nature cannot be comprehended in the narrow legalism of yesterday but in our ability to love, to be available to God and neighbour, to be mature and therefore to realise the image of God in man.

This transformation is causing a lot of anxiety in the Church as we move from one type of spirituality to another.

Manifestations in the Personality

So far I have described the symptoms of anxiety, both psychological and physical, but that leaves out the personality which carries various features of anxiety. We cannot tackle relationships in the next chapter if we are not familiar with some of the ways in which anxiety impedes the personality.

The first feature that I want to underline is that anxiety is linked with fear and one of our earliest fears is of displeasing parents and other authority figures. We can remain frightened for the rest of our lives of those who have power and, as I mentioned already, this fear can culminate in the fear of God. I said just now that the movement in our Church is from legalism to love, community and maturity. Maturation is a movement from dependence on parents to independence, self-esteem and critical evaluation. If we are going to free our energies to love, then we cannot be prisoners of our daily anxieties whether we are in a state of mortal sin or not. A lot of the spiritual energy which went in the past to appease an angry God has to be chanelled nowadays to translate his love to the members of the community.

This preoccupation with our inner world leads to the next feature of the personality that is linked with anxiety, namely the obsessional, perfectionist or scrupulous person. All these words have the same meaning; their target is different. The perfectionist is somebody who cannot leave any detail undone. I want to illustrate it in a ridiculous way but my work with marriage reminds me of this point. We must all have heard the complaint of the husband whose wife always keeps him waiting or is late for the party. This is a standard joke but it does involve the perfectionist woman, who in addition to her excuse that she has much more to do than her husband does not realise that every detail of her appearance is checked and double-checked. She is late because she never feels sure that she has got it right. There is always a lingering feeling that something can be improved. Her husband is shouting and she is agitated as she changes yet one more detail of her appearance. But this caricature of the obsessional woman has

140

its counterpart in men who dictate letters and change them a dozen times, cross-question everybody about the little details and are never satisfied with what they have done. They check and counter-check and drive everybody mad with their fussiness.

The scrupulous man or woman was typically, in the past, a person who could never be sure that they had been forgiven, that they had lost their guilt or that they had confessed all their sins. They went repeatedly back to confession and to different priests, all without avail. This scrupulosity has its secular counterpart when a patient becomes obsessed with thoughts, ideas or actions, such as washing their hands, and they will not stop for hours. I said earlier on that anxiety becomes an illness when its intensity or duration becomes severe and a point is reached when obsessionality is an illness.

Fear has been referred to as the key to anxiety and, in spiritual matters, the fear of God as a substitute parental figure gives a sense of distant awe. But the frightened or phobic personality may have other fears. The fear of open spaces or agoraphobia, or of closed spaces or claustrophobia, are familiar and common. But when it comes to relationship there are fears of getting close to people, the fear of being vulnerable, of being rejected, of saying the wrong thing, of appearing foolish. As we have seen earlier all these fears relate to self-esteem and the anxiety that one is unworthy of the love of others. At a deeper level one has the feeling that one needs to be perfect in all ways in order to present oneself to one's neighbour. Such fears lead to isolation.

Finally there is the hysteric personality. We are all afraid of being called hysterical which somehow suggests that we are second-class citizens. The notion of hysterical is confused with histrionic. The histrionic person exaggerates, dramatises, expands, has to be heard, is acting and needs attention. Often such a person is a grown-up child who is craving for excitement and attention. But the hysterical personality is someone whose anxiety has reached such a peak that there is a dissociation between mind and body or the mind does not function properly. In the latter case, one can lose one's memory or travel for long distances without remembering who one is or where is one's home, a state called a fugue. The dissociation between mind and body can lead to a paralysis of a limb which recovers when the anxiety is removed. In all these situations the anxiety overwhelms the person, and he or she responds by losing a function of their person.

I am often asked whether people with stigmata are not showing hysterical manifestations. A special feature of hysteria is that the patient is looking for relief of his anxiety, even though at times he or she appears to be totally indifferent to the outcome. In other words, hysterics have something to gain. Some of those who experience stigmata may have the same psychological make-up as hysterics but their 'gain' is really a transformation of spiritual values and their manifestations may be genuine.

Cause of Anxiety

What causes anxiety? Psychiatrists are familiar with this question and there are some standard replies. First of all some people are born predisposed to anxiety; in other words they have a genetic loading towards it. Studies of twins have shown this predilection but it is not the whole story. We can also become conditioned to anxiety. There is a very respectable personality theory of Eysenck which divides people into extroverts and introverts. Extroverts condition poorly whereas introverts condition easily and have a more anxious make-up. Finally there are a whole host of reasons in the process of our development, that is to say how trustworthy our environment is in the form of our parents. I refer to this again in chapter fourteen.

Frequency of Anxiety

Anxiety can thus be seen to be a universal characteristic. It is variously calculated that between twenty and thirty per cent of people, but more often women, need to see their doctor about it at least once in their lives. What does this high figure tell us about anxiety?

It is certainly a symptom which is very common today. Is it common because we diagnose it more often or are there other reasons? Let us examine these other reasons.

One possible feature is the gradual maturation of human beings. In the past when we had a marked dependence on figures of authority, the anxious person went to their priest, doctor, lawyer or wise friend and received reassurance. Today the priest and religion are no longer used, the doctor has no time to listen; only the wise friend remains. But even more subtly, people have grown up to the point where they do not want to be dependent on a figure of authority. They want to trust their own judgment. This desire is highly laudable but many people are left in a transition between emerging as independent persons and yet not fully secure enough in themselves. There is, therefore, a need for help in a way that respects the independence of the person. The whole range of counselling tries to do that but traditional confession does not give this impression and so, in fact, confession is out of favour.

But there may be other reasons for increased anxiety. As man explores the technological possibilities around him, so vast new possibilities emerge, but these possibilities hide dangers in them, such as nuclear war, the devastation of the environment and pollution. All this is happening at a time when God and religion are being abandoned. The world is a creation of God and its development an alliance between man and God. If God is ignored, then anxiety is bound to rise as the major partner is ignored in the way the world is to be explored.

The first sin of man was the temptation to become like God and this temptation has never ceased to attract mankind, but with it goes an anxiety of uncertainty and the world is full of it today.

I want to conclude with a word about the treatment of anxiety. We have now reached the stage where we can suppress the symptoms of anxiety with tranquillisers and Valium has become a household name, but we are now beginning to question this policy. Should not people have the right to experience anxiety and to grow through it? Is it always a good thing to suppress the manifestations of anxiety? Clearly not. For some people anxiety is a healthy event from which we learn something new about controlling our lives. For others it is an insupportable burden which crushes them and needs relief. Each person is unique and has to be responded to as such.

I have already mentioned that introverts condition easily and are more anxious. For some patients deconditioning is the answer to their problem. Deconditioning has moved fast over the last twenty-five years and much can be done in this way; I refer passingly here to dynamic growth; that is to say the development of our personality from anxiety to freedom from fear, which is dealt with in chapter fourteen.

But finally anxiety has to deal with survival and Christianity is a faith that deals with the whole cosmos which is seen as God's gift to man. In the end our faith must be a protection against anxiety. I do not mean that our faith will remove anxiety but that it will act as a partner in dialogue with anxiety. At certain times in the last hundred years Roman Catholicism has given the impression that it knows all the answers to problems. Today we recognise that this lust for certainty was wrongly serviced. Jesus Christ did not come to this world to remove anxiety but to answer it and, in the end, man cannot cope with anxiety without this spiritual dimension.

14

Anxiety and Love

Defences against Anxiety

I want to start by referring to one of Freud's great discoveries; namely that we put up psychological defences against anxiety and this has important repercussions for human relationships. The point about these defences is that they are unconscious, we do not know that we are taking this particular stance and so we earnestly believe in what we are saying but people do not believe us, do not appreciate that we are putting up a defence and condemn us. Let me illustrate this with some examples.

First we have the common defence of denial. In this situation we are often confronted with an accusation which sets up a great deal of anxiety. We can consciously lie or we can deny the accusation, honestly believing that we are not responsible for the issue in question. We do this by the process of suppression. We simply remove the facts from consciousness and we do not remember them. In the process of an exchange our friend or enemy will certainly accuse us of lying. We are in a position that we not only have to defend ourselves from the anxiety of the original problem but we now have to defend ourselves from the accusation of being liars. The exchange becomes far removed from the original issue and develops into a protracted argument about honesty and integrity which alienates the couple from each other.

Or the exchange can take a different form. Right at the very beginning it may be appreciated that the person is on the defensive, that their denial is an expression of worry and uncertainty. They can be assured of our good intentions, namely that what we want is the truth and not the accusation and condemnation of the other. In other words, the loving exchange is to create an atmosphere where the other's anxiety can be recognised and related to the events that are being denied. The truth is reached, the relationship is preserved and love can flow again.

The next common defence is projection, a process whereby we invest another with a feeling we possess, usually a bad feeling. So we are not liars but they are; we are not deceivers but they are; we are not unjust but they are, and so on. Projection can take place commonly in situations whereby our feelings about ourselves become so intolerable that we have to unload them on to others. These feelings are set in the world of badness and guilt. Usually the exchange is about trivial matters such as 'You are always late'; 'Look who is talking'; 'You are always untidy'; 'I have yet to see tidiness from you'. This process of mutual accusation goes on in families day in, day out. But it may become more serious as the other is accused of deception, sexual infidelity, arrogance, nastiness, and so on.

Projection can soon destroy mutual relations of love as the exchange becomes once again an inventory of mutual accusations. Each accusation brings a counter-attack and a vicious circle of badness is established. But like the defence of denial, projection has to be handled in a way that gives the possibility of reconciliation. It is more difficult when people accuse us of some adverse quality; we are not so keen to make allowances for their feelings. We feel angry at the accusation and we want to protect ourselves against it. But forgiveness does not here involve restoring the goodness of the person who has offended us but creating the conditions for realising that the accusation is a projection, and what the person needs is enough love to reduce their anxiety, to admit their self-rejecting feelings and move in the direction of restoring love for themselves which will reduce the need for projection.

The third defence which is common is rationalisation. In this defence the inherent anxiety about being right transforms emotional reasons into rational ones. As normally experienced we produce so-called 'reasons' for what are after all our feelings and a good deal of these feelings are the anxiety of being right. In this exchange it is difficult to get to the root of an

146

exchange because feelings are not acknowledged and reasons are substituted. This is an extremely frustrating situation in which one person is trying once again to get to the truth and the other is offering 'reasons' instead of feelings. Such exchanges can become sterile. It is vital to create an atmosphere where the feelings of the person concerned can be expressed without fear.

In all these defences the exchange is between persons but there are defences such as suppression and repression where anxiety is removed from consciousness within the individual and so it is not possible to reach intrapersonal integrity unless somebody helps us to recover our unconscious mechanisms.

It is no exaggeration to say that, deliberate deception apart, the presence of defences is the most distorting factor in exchanges of love because real trust cannot be established between two people. All the energy is spent in coping with the mutual accusations, leaving no possibility for the creation of a loving exchange.

Autonomy

These defences are established in the process of growth which in turn exposes all of us to one of the basic anxieties of our life. This anxiety is connected with the framework of our separation from our parents. The sense of oneness with which we start life has to give way to a separation in which we fashion a separate 'I' from the 'thou' of our mother and father. This is a gradual process which takes place infinitely slowly at the beginning of life and then more rapidly later on.

The first sign of anxiety at separation is physical and this continues throughout life. We need company to retain our humanity; the isolated person who flees from human contact is often disturbed. Most of us need the presence of a friend or a spouse, in particular when we are frightened, sick or worried. At these times we long to make contact with those with whom we feel safe. In technical jargon, we regress to our earlier age and need the comfort that is appropriate to it.

But when we are not in special need we have to balance our closeness with people with the distance which suits us. Most of us get this balance right but at times we find that friends who are anxious cling to us and then we have a problem of how to handle this situation. Clearly if they are in distress we have to be available for a period of time until they emerge from their panic. In other words, our task is to remain available until they overcome their distress.

The second sign of our anxiety at separation is psychological. Now the problem is no longer physical proximity but emotional trust. We have to feel secure that the other understands us correctly. Most of us are accustomed to unconditional acceptance and understanding by our parents and we look for the same penetrating awareness in adult life. This security of trust allows us to get close to people. If we do not find it, we withdraw and isolate ourselves.

Our friends can draw close to us with backgrounds which are not secure. They may have had insecure backgrounds in their childhoods and are drawn towards us for healing purposes, in order to gain security for the first time. When we undertake this role we have to be very loving and patient. Our friend is drawn to us and then finds that in real life we are not as perfect as they expect us to be. At that point they withdraw, feeling once again rejected in life. We must persist as they test us again and again, until they realise we can be trusted but we are not perfect. This may take a long time until the right feelings are established.

So far what I have said amounts to the fact that, as adults, we want our autonomy, we want to be self-directing and yet we are anxious about our loneliness; yet if we remain too close to another person we are afraid of being suffocated by them. Another way of looking at this critical issue of loving is to talk about dependence. We talk about mature dependence and immature dependence. In mature dependence we rely on the support of other people but if they disappear from our life we will not collapse with anxiety. In immature dependence the withdrawal of the other person means our collapse into a state of high anxiety. The dependent-independent dimension is one we all have to handle in our lives and it is often governed by the level of anxiety we are experiencing. As I said, none of us is totally independent, that is to say, lives without friends. But there are some people who get so anxious at being hurt by intimacy that they assume a stubborn independence which gives the appearance of 'I don't need anyone'. When we meet such a person we need to assume once again a healing role to make it possible for such a person to draw close to us without the dread of being hurt: to accept our presence without feeling they have to be helpless children and without the fear of being humiliated.

There are two other roles which we play with one another when we have not got the balance of relationship clear. If we are afraid of being hurt we assume not only the position of total aloofness but also that of total strength. Such a person is saying that he is too powerful to be hurt. Whatever anyone can do he can do it better, and so once again he does not need anyone. He is immune from hurt. Unfortunately nobody can immunise themselves from internal hurts of self-deception, the fear of being unlovable and unwanted and such a person needs as much healing as the previous one.

Finally I refer to another point of insufficient independence, that is the man or woman who is terribly needy and at the same time unsure of being wanted. Such men and women go about trying to be submissive and pleasing so they can feel accepted in return. In many ways they are begging for acceptance by offering constant placation. Very often such a person feels extremely frustrated and angry underneath their desire to be nice. They feel unlovable in their heart of hearts and their efforts to gain approval are geared to the knowledge that they would be dismissed if they were their true selves. Such wounded people also need to feel wanted for their own sake and our task is to show them unconditional acceptance.

Needless to say the process of healing not only involves the desire to love and our patient availability but also the understanding that all these wounded persons are going to treat us as the parents who hurt them in the course of their development. We must be prepared to be treated positively and negatively several times before a secure relationship is established.

Healer

Let me say a little more about the role of the healer. Hurt people will find their way to us because they will read signals of acceptance in us. They will have experienced a childhood in which mother or father were inconsistent in their upbringing, giving rise to a lot of anxiety about acceptance. They received feelings of being unwanted, unappreciated, easily abandoned, feeling unlovable and hurt. They come to us with a high level of anxiety and they want us to give them a second opportunity. They have to learn to trust us and that means we have to be consistent. We must not say one thing one moment and another the next. Consistency means that we can become reliable.

If we are to become reliable we must also be honest. We must not promise more than we can deliver. Such people will press us for signs of love, in which case we have to give what we can. If they feel unlovable they may be very reserved and wait for us to take the lead. As I have already mentioned, we are going to be watched continuously for any sign that we are behaving like their parents. We must be prepared for such a person to withdraw, to be angry and to want immediate attention. They are living in a world of constant anxiety that things can never change and their unconscious is out to prove that our efforts to love are not genuine. The work of the healer is persistence, the willingness to start again for the umpteenth time and to be genuinely loving, which means to recognise the hurt of the individual but to offer seriously an alternative. This alternative is not believed in the beginning but gradually the wounded person experiences a different atmosphere and their feelings change from anxiety to security, from rejection to acceptance.

Love and Anger

In the process of healing, both the wounded and the healers will experience anger and it is time to look at the relationship between anxiety and anger. The most basic and general connection comes from the fact that anxiety sets up a situation in which we are alerted to danger. One reaction has to be to fight or to flee and anger mobilises the energy to do either. Now let us look at the human situation.

As already described, when we are very young our experience is that of love, and yet both as infants and children we do things that are aggressive and elicit the anger of our parents, which in turn makes us anxious at displeasing them.

150

As babies we bite the breast, as toddlers we damage and break things. The result is a shout and we get alarmed. But we get more than alarmed, for at that moment of anxiety we feel guilty and bad. Our notions of being good and bad arise from the way we are treated and the anger we receive and later on our anger will become part of the moments when we rebel against the love of our parents. Thus love and anger become an intrinsic part of our life and are related to anxiety.

Its intrinsic nature really means that we cannot have a close relationship with anybody without experiencing love and anger towards them and anxiety in ourselves. Ambivalence is a situation of struggle for the rest of our lives. Whenever we love we shall find ourselves in a position to be angry and therefore the challenge in our life is that our love becomes greater than our anger. How can we do this?

I think we cannot escape being angry when our anger is about something critical in the relationship. Anger is a signal of threat and, if the relationship is threatened, then we must be angry and let the other person know. But anger has to be distinguished from being destructive. In the process of destruction we want to eliminate the other; in anger we want to warn them that we are anxious about something we consider serious. If a relationship is to be honest, then genuine feelings must be expressed.

At this point I am often asked whether it is possible to sustain a relationship if we are angry with each other every five minutes. The answer is that we have to distinguish between trivial irritations and anxieties that we have to absorb and major threats that need to be faced.

Clearly we are not always going to be right when we are angry and the chances of misinterpreting the behaviour of other people is high. Thus we are going to be angry in situations when our anger is not justified. What do we do then? Both in the name of love and justice we have to apologise and make reparation and this is what is often done. Sometimes however, depending on our childhood experiences, we find it difficult to apologise because we feel we will not be forgiven or in the process we will be humiliated or our feelings of badness will be confirmed. So we do not apologise; instead we sulk. There are people who cannot apologise and have always to be rescued by their partner who has to make the first move.

At this point I want to draw attention to a well known psychological fact which we find in the Epistles of St John directly related to our theme. The point I want to make is that loving is more important than expressing anger even though the latter is a response to the anxiety of survival. Anger nevertheless makes us fear the loss of approval of those who love us and the reception of punishment, so that we refrain from being angry or we remain in fear that we cannot be in a state of honesty and integrity. Fear is really incompatible with love and that is precisely what St John says.

> God is love
> and anyone who lives in love lives in God,
> and God lives in him.
> Love will come to its perfection in us
> when we can face the day of Judgment without fear;
> because even in this world
> we have become as he is.
> In love there can be no fear
> but fear is driven out by perfect love:
> because to fear is to expect punishment
> and anyone who is afraid is still imperfect in love.
>
> (1 John 4:16–18)

Having moved to the scriptures, I want to take two more examples about anxiety which are fundamental in our faith. The first deals with the relationship of trust between Jesus and his Father. It would take several pages of quotations to show the trust that our Lord had in his Father which the dialogues of John bring out clearly and unequivocally. Jesus had a profound awareness of his Father from the age of twelve in the Temple until the time of his death, when he delivered his spirit to him. But, as in human relationships, this trust was tested in the garden of Gethsemane. Here we are told that 'sadness came over him and great distress'. 'My soul is sorrowful to the point of death' (Matthew 26:37–8). He sweated drops of blood and he undoubtedly exhibited a great deal of anxiety. This was an important moment for him. He could follow the road to Calvary, the road of love, or turn back. In the case of our Lord, the choice was not between anger and love, love and not loving, but between obedience to love and obedience to betrayal. Our Lord went on to the love of absolute trust and that trust led to his death and resurrection. We too have to make countless choices for and against love of God and neighbour as we build and wander through relationships. Since the kingdom of God has begun, we have to move forward in love in the way Jesus did.

But this trust of Jesus's was not suddenly built in the garden of Gethsemane. It grew gradually over time and I want to quote the marvellous passage from Luke:

Then he said to the disciples: This is why I am telling you not to worry about your life and what you are to eat, nor about your body and how you are to clothe it. For life means more than food and the body more than clothing. Think of the ravens. They do not sow or reap; they have no storehouses and no barns; yet God feeds them. And how much more are you worth than the birds! Can any of you, for all his worrying, add a single cubit to his span of life? . . . Think of the flowers; they never have to spin or weave, yet I assure that not even Solomon in all his regalia was robed like one of these. Now if that is how God clothes the grass in the field which is here today and thrown in the furnace tomorrow, how much more will he look after you, you men of little faith! But you, you must not set your hearts on things to eat and things to drink nor must you worry. It is the pagans of the world who set their hearts on all these things. Your Father well knows you need them. No; set your hearts on his kingdom, and these other things will be given you as well. There is no need to be afraid, little flock, for it has pleased your Father to give you the kingdom. (Luke 12: 22–32)

What a supreme pronouncement of confidence in his Father. What a measure of reassurance for us. In this beautiful and symbolic language Jesus is really giving us a major lesson of faith. The Father knows our needs and, if we were to spend the minimum time on our needs and the major part of our life loving, then we are set for the kingdom of God!

Growth

This leads me to the final point, namely the growth from anxiety to freedom. The removal of anxiety may be achieved by ourselves or with the help of others. Usually the process combines both approaches. We need to replace the moments of anxiety with trust and that means trusting ourselves and our neighbour. You may well say that in any age trusting your neighbour is a dangerous thing. We have to do what our Lord did, which is to place one hand forward and show trust and the other behind, monitoring the response. We must never cease making efforts to trust ourselves and others, and at the same time never stop correcting, amending, changing, so that we do not deceive ourselves, deceive others or be deceived by them. But the day that anxiety replaces trust we have lost our way.

Within a framework of trust, we have to believe that no offence is unforgivable, no expression of anger unpardonable, and this has to be mutual. If love is to flourish we must have the freedom to be angry without the fear of retaliation or rejection and that is, of course, how we have to behave in return.

Just as we must have the freedom to be angry without fear, so we must learn to live with some doubt. There is a hunger for certainty, some would call it lust. But the only certainty we can have is that of faith which, in turn, is immersed in mystery. We live constantly between the brightness of certainty and the shadow of anxiety and doubt. That is how life is constructed. Our hunger for certainty can only be met as we join the quest of our Lord but that quest wll only be completed in the resurrection. In the meantime we live between faith and doubt which can only be bridged by love. Love brings God into existence. It does not remove anxiety or doubt but it transforms them from fear into companions of living, making them safe.

The presence of trust, the freedom of expressing anger and the toleration of doubt allow us to remove the masks from our personality. We don't have to pretend in our relationships. We can show ourselves as we are, hurt, wounded, imperfect but never ceasing to try to overcome our fears and move towards loving ourselves and others. If we are genuine, then we can treat others genuinely; that is to say with spontaneity, warmth and empathy. We don't have to pretend that we are devoid of anxieties. If we share our pain with others, then we enter into a mutuality of confidence and we can go on growing.

If we do this, we move from fear to love. If fear means destruction and running away, love means creation and movement towards others. If anxiety means uncertainty, then love means certainty that we want and are wanted.

If anxiety means vacillation, then love means persistence. If anxiety means suspicion, then love means security. If anxiety means anger, then love means affirmation.

In the creation of this world God made himself available through love and not through doubt and offered the certainty of his only Son. In our creativity we too have to make ourselves ready through love to reduce the anxiety in ourselves and in this way make ourselves available to stem the anxiety that destroys others.

Anxiety spans a bridge of survival on the one part and the freedom from fear to the certainty of love on the other. We are all crossing the bridge and the kingdom of God is the path that is marked love.

Postscript

At the end of the book readers will have reached their own conclusion whether the material is useful to their own lives or not. The subjects chosen for discussion are among the most common themes in personal relationships, but they do not exhaust the possible range of topics which can be examined. And so in this postscript I want to leave readers with some insight about the way to go on tackling by themselves further issues. I want to place this thought against the background of living in our age.

All of us are familiar with the gradual emptying of the churches and the spirit of secularism that has replaced a life of faith. There is in all of us a need for immediacy and certainty, and science appears to give us both. The mystery of the cosmos is being answered by astronomy, the wonder of the body, by medicine. The very depths of the origin of life are brought under human control. Everywhere there seems to be an answer and yet all that science does is to enlighten the creation of life; in no way do its answers replace the ultimate need for a loving creator. Understanding how things work does not tell us the reasons why they exist. Religion is wedded to the why of life. That why is found in the Christian revelation in the life, death and resurrection of Jesus Christ who is the image of the unseen God and is in fact love. The answer of Christianity to the secularity of science is not to try and compete with it, but to complete it with love in our daily life.

This life is moving imperceptibly into recognising the depths of relationship. This is the relationship between nations, between societies and above all between people. In the 'I'–'thou' encounter we not only meet our neighbour but also the love of God and, through this, God himself.

But how do we bring about this love? Whatever the experience concerned we have to recognise that what is needed is to mobilise the fullness of our being, physical, emotional, intellectual and spiritual, and to reach our neighbour with this potential. In particular, we have to recognise the role that feelings and emotions play in our life and the life of others, and when we are in tune, aware of our body, mind and feelings, we proceed to ask what would Christ do in these circumstances. We embrace the whole of our human experience ultimately in the experience of Christ. Hence, throughout this book the human experience is seen in the light of the divine counterpart.

Having become as fully aware of ourselves as possible, we need to receive the other by listening as attentively as possible to their needs. Once again the communication has to extend beyond an intellectual grasp. We have to identify the feelings of the other person and respond to them accurately in their pain or joy, fear or security, anger or peace.

This love, which is the sign of the Christian life, is the affirmative mobilisation of self with the purpose of being available to our neighbour, minute by minute in life. This availability in love is something that science cannot give and Christianity can. But in order to realise it we have to use all the dimensions of our humanity including the psychological ones.

This book has attempted to do precisely this and the various expositions are meant to act as a pointer to the realisation of love in other human situations.

Index

achievement 75, 81
adolescence 53, 82–4
affirmation 60–1, 134, 155, 157
aggression 39–40, 77–9; and
  image of God 113–24, love
  125–35, self 125–7; benign
  113–14, 117–19; biological
  basis 116–17, 125; destructive
  119–21, 128; human 117;
  innate 114–15; reactive
  115–16; towards oneself
  130–3
ambivalence 79–80, 83, 151
anger 39–40, 77–9, 125; and
  destruction 128–9, guilt
  127–8; expression of 39–40,
  129–30; God's 121, 125;
  towards self 130–3
anxiety 95–7; and love 145–55,
  personality 140–2; cause of
  142; defences against 145–7;
  frequency of 142–3;
  manifestations 136, 140–2;
  meaning of 136–44; physical
  characteristics of 136–8;
  purpose of 138–40;
  treatment of 143–4
Aristotle 2
attachment 35, 49–52, 71–4
availability 27, 33–4, 49, 72
authority 35, 118–19; meaning
  of 23–4; of Jesus 24–5

autonomy 13–14, 35, 51, 147–9
awareness 7–10, 98

Barth, Karl 5
Bowlby, John 49

Cairn, David, *The Image of God*
  10
change 40–2, 107–8
child-parent relationship 13–16,
  18–19, 35–6, 38–4, 48–53,
  71–9 *passim*, 81, 106, 127,
  131, 147, 150–1; registering
  others 37–8
Christ: affirmation 60,
  aggression 121–4, authority
  24–5, availability 34, 49,
  fullness 21–2, identity 27,
  possession of self 49, 131,
  presence of Father 37,
  rejection 103, separateness,
  26–7, suffering 109–12, trust
  152–5
Christian experience 108–12
closeness 36, 51, 71, 87, 100,
  120, 148
commitment 41, 59–60
communication 37–8, 42–5, 50,
  65–6, 88–90
competence 15, 75
continuity 18, 40–2, 59, 73
criticism 61, 102–3

159